# ILLUSIONS

Shed Lies // Embrace Truth // Experience Joy

## BILL GIOVANNETTI

Endurant Press

ISBN E-book edition: 978-1-946654-07-6

ISBN Print edition: 978-1-946654-04-5

Cover by jgraphics.com

For additional resources, please visit maxgrace.com.

# CONTENTS

# ILLUSIONS

Therefore whoever hears these sayings of Mine, and does them, I will liken him to a wise man who built his house on the rock: and the rain descended, the floods came, and the winds blew and beat on that house; and it did not fall, for it was founded on the rock. But everyone who hears these sayings of Mine, and does not do them, will be like a foolish man who built his house on the sand: and the rain descended, the floods came, and the winds blew and beat on that house; and it fell. And great was its fall. (Matthew 7:24-27)

Our world runs on illusions. Most of the rules that make our society go are messed up. They damage the human soul. They contradict long-proven logic. They break hearts. And, above all, they essentially tell God to take a hike.

The rules we all play by every single day have built a giant house on sinking sand.

An illusion is something that seems to be real but isn't. It seems to be true but it's false. Sometimes, is enormously difficult to tell what is real from what is unreal. So much of what we think is true isn't true. It is unreality. It is an illusion.

Odds are strong you have been deceived.

Brainwashed.

Fooled.

It's time to start building your house on the rock.

I want to help you break free of the illusions that limit your life. I want to show you, from God's Word, how to escape the matrix of self-defeating delusions and self-exalting fantasies. I'm passionate about helping you elude the lies, dodge the deceptions, and sidestep the untruths and the half-truths that everybody just assumes to be true, but in the end cause nothing but heartbreak and pain.

An illusion contradicts reality.

You can't fight reality and win. Contradicted Reality Always Zaps You. It's C.R.A.Z.Y. The devil's lies damage relationships, infect you with guilt, frustrate your plans, and break your heart.

— C.R.A.Z.Y. — CONTRADICTED
REALITY ALWAYS ZAPS YOU

Just as you can't violate the law of gravity without becoming a splat on the sidewalk, so you can't violate God's laws of reality without consequences. Yet the illusions of the world convince you to try.

What if we have been sucked into a matrix of lies? What if there is a systematic effort to brainwash whole societies and cultures, and to convince us all of lies? And what if much of that brainwashing is sincere, and well-meaning, and well-intentioned?

A lie is still a lie even if the motives are good.

Let's lay out some basic premises of this book.


## BASIC PREMISES

*1. We believe that Christianity is one, huge, beautiful truth that begins in the heart of God.*

It is consistent with science, because science began in the heart of God too. It is consistent with mathematics, because mathematics began in the heart of God too. The Christian truth is consistent with history, logic, philosophy, ethics, art, and medicine. Every subject of science and knowledge is in perfect harmony with the Christian message, because all truth came from the same source.

All truth is God's truth.

When you build your life on God's truth, the house on the rock stands firm.

But not all that claims to be true is true, and this is what makes our world so messed up. This is where pain comes from, heartbreak comes from, and violence comes from.

---

2. *The World System is a collection of fragmented, disconnected, contradictory illusions masquerading as truth.*

Yes, the prevailing world-philosophy offers some truth, but it is partial. It is distorted. It is pieced together in the wrong way.

Besides, it is plagued by a shaky foundation utterly inadequate to sustain an abundant life.

Before I state that shaky foundation, a story. Some time ago, I was driving in my car in my then hometown of Chicago, and listening to a late night radio show called "Extension 720." The host, Milt Rosenburg, was an engaging conversationalist and a professor of psychology at the University of Chicago. He interviewed three guests, that night. They were astrophysicists and their topic was the origin of the universe. It was a fascinating conversation.

At one point, the host asked a question that brought the conversation to a screeching halt.

He said, "I have noticed that many physicists and scientists like yourself do not believe in God. Why do you think that is?"

As I said, the question brought the conversation to a halt. There I was, driving the windswept streets on a late and frigid Chicago night. Nobody was around. It was a memorable moment. I leaned into my radio because I really wanted to hear this answer.

After an awkward silence, one of the scientists spoke up. He said, "To be really honest, Milt, I think the main reason most of us don't believe in God is because if there were a god, we would have to change the way we live, and most of us don't want to do that."

What did I just hear?

Thank you for being honest. Thank you for not burying the true intent of your atheism. I respect that position, even as I disagree with it.

This is the fatal infection of the world's most basic philosophy: *The world shifts its version of truth to justify whatever lifestyle it prefers.*

That is precisely how to build your life on shifting sand. And, in turn, that is precisely how you set yourself up for collapse.

The method of the world-system is to bypass the mind in order to hypnotize the heart. Once it has the heart, it creates a seemingly logical structure, but it is, in realty, built on crumbling substructures. It is built on lies. Or to use the words of Jesus, it doesn't matter how seemingly logical, popular, sensible, beautiful a system is, if it is a house built on sand, it will fall.

These illusions come from being convinced that

a lie is the truth, and then acting that conviction out. It comes from being sucked into the matrix of unreality.

The brainwashing that comes at us every single day is committed to pulling us away from the eternal truths of God into a quagmire of half-truths and deceptions, even as it paints its lies in breathtaking hues.

---

*3. We are not free to modify God's truth when it is unpopular or repellent to the world.*

The sum of Christian teaching is one big truth-package; don't mess with it. We have not been called to move people from one illusion to another illusion. We have been called to guide them out of the matrix. In Christianity, we are empowered to cast aside the ever-changing illusions, and to summon the world to build their lives on the solid rock of Jesus Christ.

People say they don't like Christianity. So be it. Let's not be jerks about that fact. Let's be sure we're not getting in the way because we're, well, idiots. Let's be real. I've been around Christians a whole lot. And some of us are just plain weird.

Even so, the message of the Bible isn't up for a vote. Even if people don't like it.

It is not our mission to soften the offense of the gospel — which begins with, "Hi my name is Bill, and you're a sinner, and you need a Savior." That offense is never going away, regardless of what language we use.

Nor is the answer simply to bury the gospel under an avalanche of good deeds done in Jesus' name. Fixing the world, healing diseases, helping mankind — these are fantastic causes and we participate in them, and we should — but they are only part of the Church's mission to the degree that they open up doors to actually helping people find God and then follow God.

I can give you ten thousand cups of cold water, but if I never tell you about Jesus, you will still be spiritually thirsty. As a friend and missionary who has built hospitals in the world's poorest lands has asked — a man who has spent a lifetime training surgeons to serve in impoverished places in Africa — has said, "What good is it if we heal the body but the soul spends eternity far from God?"

Christianity's hard truths are not negotiable. They are part of a beautiful, self-authenticating truth-package that flows from the heart of God, and the only reason any one would want to change it is because we don't know what beauty is. This is because our hearts have been infected. We've been brainwashed. Down is up, and evil is good, and wrong is right, and ugly is art.

If any part of the glorious interlocking truth and reality package that is called the Gospel of Grace, and the Truth of Christianity — if any part of that looks anything but beautiful the only reason is because there is something wrong in the eye of the beholder. This truth flows from the heart of God. It is glorious, and wondrous, and beautiful, and good. It is real. It defines reality.

So if you don't like the biblical message, pause. Don't jump to conclusions. Ask what's wrong, and don't assume you're in the right. Dig deeply. Go beyond the surface. Be very sure you don't modify God's truth. Instead, modify yourself.

Shed the illusion.

Escape the matrix.

# HUMANISM

Please do not confuse *humanism* with *humanitarianism*. Humanitarianism means caring for people, and as Christians, we are fans of that.

Humanism is something different. It is, ultimately, a worldview painfully out of sync with reality.

## WHAT IS HUMANISM?

*Humanism is a philosophy of life that puts humans at the pinnacle of existence.*

There is an organization called the American Humanist Association. Their motto is "Good without a god." Humanists say that Reason and Science are all we need to create a just and good society. In fact, they say, it is religion that gets in the way. This is because religion always leads to superstition, and superstition always brings us backwards. Humanism almost always goes hand in hand with atheism.

If humans are at the top of existence, they are either higher than God, or there is no God. We humans—with our philosophies and values—occupy the top rung of the existential ladder. You might hear the term, *secular* humanism, because *secular* means the opposite of sacred. It means a world without reference to God, or faith, or the supernatural. Secular humanism stands against anything that rises above matter and energy and science and reason and the space-time continuum. Secular humanism is atheism organizing itself into an "unreligion" and working to evangelize the world.

Since 1933 there has been a humanist "manifesto." You can find it online. It's now in its third edition. Here is what humanists say about themselves:

> *Humanism is a progressive philosophy of life that, without supernaturalism, affirms our ability and responsibility to lead ethical lives of personal fulfillment that aspire to the greater good of humanity.*

Don't miss the operative words: "without supernaturalism."

Here are some famous humanists. If you enjoy science fiction, you'll know the names Isaac Asimov, Kurt Vonnegut, and Gene Roddenberry (created *Star Trek*). For astronomy, there's Carl Sagan, author of *The Cosmos*. For political activists, there is Jack Kevorkian (aka Dr. Death), Gloria Steinem, Karl Marx, and Barney Frank. In the media, Oliver Stone... it's a long list of accomplished people.

Let's break down humanism's essence point by point.

## SOME FEATURES OF HUMANISM

*EVOLUTION. Humans are the products of evolution.*

Humanists don't just apply the theory of evolution to our biology, they also apply it to our sociology and psychology. Perhaps this is because they see a material (i.e., made of matter) cause for basically everything — even our passions and loves.

As we continue to evolve, the world and society will keep getting better and better, or so the humanist idea goes.

One huge sticking point is that it simply isn't happening. Violence isn't going away. Corruption isn't going away. Man's inhumanity to man isn't going away. Humanism's core proposition is manifestly unreal.

Furthermore, think of humanism this way: to make evolution the driving principle of your cultural system is to create a whole society based on survival of the fittest.

How is survival of the fittest as a core philosophy going to make the world a more compassionate place? Isn't compassion for the vulnerable and weak the opposite of survival of the fittest? Shouldn't we just take out the weak, and help evolution along?

That is exactly where dedicated humanists go in their thinking. The elderly. The infirm. Those with certain handicaps. Infants. The unborn. They are pulling down the species so they just have to go.

In Iceland recently there has been a movement to abort all Down Syndrome babies. What is this, but humans making the world a colder, crueler place in the name of improving the gene pool.

It isn't humanism; it's in-humanism.

Evolution is making the world a better place, they say. But it isn't. So how do humanists answer that?

They answer by pointing to the people who might be reading this book. They blame you. Christians. God-oriented, superstitious, backward, narrow-minded, bigots.

The only thing holding society back is religious people, gods, and superstition.

Religious people are anti-evolution, and so we want to bring the world backwards into things like faith in God and the Bible.

We're the problem, from the humanist perspective.

---

*PROGRESS. Faith in human nature and in human progress.*

Humans maintain we can create a just and beautiful world without God.

Humanists are very optimistic about what humans can achieve. We can create utopia. We just need to "come together." "Onward and upward" is the humanist slogan.

Never forget that "we just need to come together" is code for "we must eradicate the opposing view."

There is a humanist hymn — a massively long poem by Charles Swinburne — from the late 1800s. Here are the closing lines:

> Thou art smitten, thou God, thou art
>     smitten;
> Thy death is upon thee, O Lord.
> And the love-song of earth as
>     thou diest
> Resounds through the wind of
>     her wings—
> Glory to Man in the highest!
> For Man is the master of things.

They hate it when we say this, but humanism is a religion, and it is worshipping a corrupt deity.

---

*TEMPORARINESS. We have only one life, and after this life is over, there is nothing.*

No heaven, no hell, no prayer, no special meaning, nothing at all. It's over.

No hope, no love, no peace. Just biological imperatives.

According to the humanist mindset, for Christians to teach salvation is to give people a false hope. We're messing with people's minds. It's so much better to just tell the truth, and to say that there is no heaven, and there is no hell.

Which is another way of saying that all the bad guys get away with it, and evil wins in the end, but that's for another talk. Humanists call Christianity harmful and dangerous for speaking of an afterlife.

---

*MORAL CONVENIENCE. Humans decide what is morally right and morally wrong for themselves.*

Right and wrong are based on consensus. We all agree something is right and wrong, and that's it.

In those days there was no king in Israel;

everyone did what was right in his own eyes.
(Judges 17:6)

However humanists also say that people should think for themselves, because humans rule.

And that makes humanists very open and permissive when it comes to morality. Pretty much anything is okay between consenting people. Humans are very tolerant, except for the free expression of religion, and except for situations when people have a moral opinion against their own. Then, they run to the courts to sue the opposition out of business.

Right and wrong are based on what humans agree is right or wrong.

But what if humans agree that killing Jews is right, or that slavery is right, or that racism is right? What if human consensus is wrong? Under humanism, there is no higher court of appeal because humans are the highest court of all. So the *consensus* always becomes *tyranny*. This is inevitable. It always becomes the violent overthrow of human institutions, and brother against brother, sister against sister, and everyone against God.

There is no God above, and no law of God, and nobody to answer to in the end.

This is the death of human kindness. There is no rational basis for compassion. There is no rational basis for morality, for right and wrong, other than survival of the fittest, and might makes right, under humanism.

---

SCIENCE. *Science and reason will solve the world's problems.*

Humanists say that the world will keep getting better because knowledge keeps on increasing.

The Humanist Manifesto 2 proclaims:

> Using technology wisely we can control our environment, conquer poverty, markedly reduce disease, extend our life-span, significantly modify our behavior, alter the course of human evolution and cultural development, unlock vast new powers, and provide humankind with unparalleled opportunity for achieving an abundant and meaningful life.

No need for faith, hope, or love. No need for God. No need for prayer. No need for anything but test tubes and scientists in lab coats and programmers.

Never mind that a century of humanist ideology hasn't made a bit of difference.

This is humanism. It is what your kids hear when they go to college and high school. It is what you see on the Internet and on TV. It is the underlying premise to music, arts, entertainment, movies, you name it.

But if Jesus is right, to build your life on humanist ideals is to build a life on sinking sand.

## HOW CAN WE ANSWER HUMANISM?

*1. We agree that human life should be HONORED, but you don't honor human life enough.*

Humanists say that humans are to be honored because of our development. We are the apex predator, the most highly evolved species, so far at least. So there is our honor. It is because of our development.

But Christians say we possess our honor for a higher and more glorious reason.

Christians say that humans possess honor and dignity and value and worth, not because of our developmental stage, but because of our *identity*. And that identity is amazing.

> Then God said, "Let Us make man in Our image, according to Our likeness; let them have dominion over the fish of the sea, over the birds of the air, and over the cattle, over all the earth and over every creeping thing that creeps on the earth." (Genesis 1:26)

We are not just the top of a natural food chain.

We are created with a supernatural origin. We are sacred. We are special to God in a way that no other species is special to God. We reflect his personhood. We reflect his intelligence. We reflect his free will.

Personhood is something granted by God at the moment life begins, i.e., at conception. It is not something granted by the collective, or given by the government, or bestowed by the elites, or justified by our usefulness to the group. Humanism makes the poor, the unfortunate, the disabled into something less than persons. It calls them a drain on society. And the Christian cries NO!

God gave us our personhood, and no one at any time has any right to take it away.

Human Life is sacred and belongs to God. Don't mess with it.

Humans are far more important and glorious than humanism gives them credit for.

---

2. *We agree that human life should be FREE, but we don't think you recognize our freedom enough.*

Humanists say that we should be free to make our own choices. Especially our own moral choices. Christians agree.

But, from the Christian perspective, humanists

don't recognize how vast and enormous human freedom really is.

For the humanist, the little machine inside that drives all our choices is some kind of biological imperative. The humanist philosophy makes us slaves of our DNA, slaves of our hormones, slaves of our addiction, and slaves of our environment.

But when we act in ways that are contrary to the beautiful truth of God, that isn't freedom. That is bondage. That is slavery. Addiction isn't freedom, it is bondage.

Unrestrained sexuality isn't freedom, it is bondage, and heartbreak, and a frustrating quest for a sense of self.

But that sense of self will never be found outside of a relationship with the Creator of Self, the Lord Jesus Christ.

There is no freedom in following the dictates of a biological machine of the human being.

True freedom is stepping into the vast playground called God's salvation, and realizing that the chains are off, and you are free to do everything that brings the human heart real joy.

Therefore if the Son makes you free, you shall be free indeed. (John 8:36)

*3. We agree that humans possess GLORY, but you don't recognize that glory enough.*

If the humanist story is correct, I am organized matter and energy. If we had the technology, we could reproduce ME, in a lab. My ideas. My individuality. My thoughts. My memories. My loves. My relationships. Just chemicals and energy bouncing around in the test tube of my brain, if the humanist story is correct.

If the biblical story is correct, I am a body, soul, and spirit. I am a convergence of three essences, built by God, and held together by him.

According to the Bible, I am glorious. I will one day be a spectacle to dazzle the angels. Right now, my glory is hidden. But one day, it will be revealed.

When Christ who is our life appears, then you also will appear with Him in glory. (Colossians 3:4)

What is man that You are mindful of him, And the son of man that You visit him? For You have made him a little lower than the angels, And You have crowned him with glory and honor. (Psalm 8:4,5)

The basic disagreement I have with humanism is simple.

*As a human being, I am much closer to an angel than I am to an ape.*

And that definition makes all the difference in the world.

---

*4. We agree that human life should be PROLONGED by science and other means, but we don't think you make it long enough.*

Humanism imprisons every individual life within the bonds of time. You are born. You live. You die. The end.

The natural result of humanism is despair. Always. Depression. Hopelessness. Giving up. After all you've lived and loved and dreamed and served, there's nothing in the end. You suffer. You die. And that's it.

It's so depressing because for the humanist, your life means nothing.

Or, if you think it means something, it's only because you've made it up.

But Christians know that death is not the end. There's another realm. Another cosmos. Another life after this life. And it is a continuation, but not a continuation. It is beautiful and perfect and good for those who are prepared. And it is sadness and brokenness and pain for those who are not.

I am going to heaven. That fact shapes the

purpose of everyday I live. And gives meaning to every thought I think.

I am a human created in the image of God. I have a destiny. And that destiny is not dust.

I am destined for a realm so magnificent that words can't do it justice. It can only be described in terms of streets of gold and gates of jewels and flowing rivers and robes of light. In that place, I will meet, face to face, the Ultimate Human, the God-man, the Lord Jesus Christ. He will embrace me. Instantly, every single moment of heartbreak and trial I dealt with on earth will be given eternal significance and meaning in heaven. This world is not my home, I'm just passing through.

Knowing that is me, escaping the matrix.

# DETERMINISM

To him who overcomes I will grant to sit with Me on My throne, as I also overcame and sat down with My Father on His throne. (Revelation 3:21)

For if by the one man's offense death reigned through the one, much more those who receive abundance of grace and of the gift of righteousness will reign in life through the One, Jesus Christ. (Revelation 5:17)

A man sits behind bars, locked up for many years to come. His horrendous crime haunts him. His soul replays it in his dreams. His mind is clouded every waking hour. His conscience strikes him with guilt. But he shakes it off. He tells himself what he has always told himself. He repeats the only message that makes him feel better about himself. The man says, "I am a victim of my circumstances. I couldn't help myself."

A woman and man share a drink after work. The small voice of conscience whispers of families waiting for mom and dad to come home, but they really have to celebrate. They have just landed a huge account, something they have worked hard to get. Now, it's time to unwind. It's time to party. A few hours later, the man has a sparkle in his eyes, and the woman has a gleam in hers, and they find themselves in a cab going home together. The next day, they tell themselves, "One thing led to another. We couldn't help ourselves."

A woman stares out the window with a blank expression on her face. Her children sit on the sofa behind her. They are crying. Again. She has vented her rage on them yet again. She feels horrible. A thousand times she has promised God she would never go off on them like that again. And a thousand times, she has failed. "I have a bad temper," she tells herself. "It's in my DNA. I can't help myself."

## I CAN'T HELP MYSELF

Every time any person says or thinks or believes "I can't help myself," they are expressing Determinism. In its extreme form, determinism says that every-thing in life is predetermined.

It sounds like this:

*"I am a determinist. I basically believe that at any one point in time it is completely the configuration of molecules in the universe and in particular in your brain that mandates what you do and that you could not have done anything other than what you did. In other words, you don't have any choices. You think you do, and it looks like you do, but you don't really."*

— DR. JERRY COYNE, PROFESSOR AT THE UNIVERSITY OF CHICAGO

"It is completely the configuration of molecules in the universe and in your brain." That is what controls everything. It is determined by biology. By science. By energy. By random chemical reactions. By a chain reaction begun eons ago, resulting in you crossing a boundary you swore you'd never cross.

Determinism has infected so much of what the world just assumes is true today. It is wrong, and depressing, and makes us limp beneath our dignity as royal children of God.

Let's break it down.

## WHAT IS DETERMINISM?

*DETERMINISM is a philosophy of life in which everything in our lives and our world is governed by physical laws of cause and effect, so that free will is only an illusion.*

Everything is caused by something else. Every relationship. Every emotion. Every belief. Every action. Everything is a chain of cause and effect. Your prayers. Your beliefs. Your loves.

These are not your choices.

These are not your beliefs.

Not your passions or your dreams.

These are nothing but the outworking of biological imperatives, and the physics of molecules and energy interacting in your brain.

Getting married. Having children. Caring for aging parents. Generosity. Kindness. Love. It's all nothing but long, complicated, linked chains of cause and effect.

In that chain, YOU are no more or less important than any other link. You are just another part of the giant chemical machine called the universe.

You are a puppet, and other forces are pulling the strings.

Determinism has a little sister called Fatalism.

---

*FATALISM IS the belief that we're stuck with what will be will be, since all events, past, present, and future, are determined by causes beyond our ability to influence.*

Greek mythology depicted three sister goddesses called the Fates. They were blind, ugly, and ancient. For every life, and every being, the Fates spun a thread. One sister spun the thread of life. One sister determined how long the thread should go. And one sister, when the time was right, cut the thread with her shears, and that was the end.

The fates were even stronger than the gods, because nobody can escape the Fates.

You might laugh at that today, but fatalism and determinism are nasty viruses that have infected so much of what most people believe today.

## WHAT ARE SOME KEY BELIEFS OF DETERMINISM?

*1. MATERIALISM. Everything is a bunch of chemical ping pong balls bouncing around in an energy soup.*

There is matter.

There is energy.

There is matter and energy together plus nothing. Every idea, every belief, and every love is a chemical reaction. The intimate motions of human relationships, and the cosmic motions of galaxies and stars are all the same.

The cosmos is all that is, or was, or ever will be. And it is nothing other than matter interacting with energy.

Therefore, under this view, the only major difference between a rock and a light bulb and a dog and a boy is how complicated of a chemistry set we are. Otherwise, we're all the same thing, and the only thing that divides us is where we land on the spectrum of complexity.

Life is not sacred.

God is not real. No miracles. No angels. No demons. No heaven. No hell.

Love is a chemistry experiment.

Life is an accident.

Existence is absurd.

And the destiny of everything is the slow-motion death of thermodynamic equalization when the cosmos burns all its fuel.

Eat, drink, and be merry, for tomorrow we die.

---

2. *NO FREE WILL. Free will and human choice are simply an illusion.*

A famous philosopher said,

> *In the mind there is no absolute or free will; but the mind is determined to wish this or that by a cause, which has also been determined by another cause, and this last by another cause, and so on to infinity.*

— BARUCH SPINOZA

There's that chain of cause and effect.

Today, you picked up this book. Other people did not pick up this book.

You made a choice.

They made a choice.

But not really.

All those choices are illusions. If determinism is true, the actual reason you picked up this book is because you were shoved here by cause and effect chains that started a million years ago.

The same holds for people who didn't pick up this book today.

A few years ago, I asked Margi to marry me. This happened a couple of weeks before Christmas.

I bought a diamond ring, and put it on an ornament, and hung it on the Christmas tree. On the big proposal night, I asked her to find that particular ornament. When she did, she saw the sparkly diamond ring. Her eyes got big. Her body shuddered. And she froze. I took that as a good sign.

She didn't even notice me sneak up behind her, and broken-foot and all, get down on one knee.

And I asked her to marry me. She got kind of blubbery and nodded her head. I asked if that meant yes, and she squeaked out a yes.

So I slipped a diamond on her finger.

I chose her.

And she chose me.

And many reading this book are married or you have been married. You chose each other.

But, actually you didn't, if determinism is true. The molecules in the test tube of your brain were shoved in a certain direction, and cause-and-effect created a million year old daisy chain, and there was absolutely no genuine choice here. I couldn't do anything BUT propose to Margi, and she couldn't do anything BUT say yes.

It was all determined, because free will is just an illusion.

Many years ago, determinism sent Margi and me from Chicago to California. Determinism sent you to wherever you are too. Determinism selects our presidents, decides our weather, strikes us with diseases, and decides who will win the World Series.

No choice. No goals. No dreams. No striving for what you believe in. No defeat if you blow it. No authentic victory if you overcome.

Just the random chance of molecular ping pong and impersonal cosmic forces playing a game with the machinery of the universe, and we're all part of the game.

It's all just a dream.

And vanity.

And chasing the wind.

*3. FLAVORS. Determinism comes in a wide variety of flavors.*

*SUPERSTITIOUS DETERMINISM. I am at the mercy of luck, the stars, my horoscope, curses, and, oops, I broke a mirror.*

Christians don't believe in being lucky or unlucky. Luck is named after the Norse God Loki, yes, Thor's brother. He was always tricky and always causing trouble.

The Bible is also clear that a curse has no power over your life.

We believe our lives are in the hand of a caring and powerful Father in heaven, and he has a name, and he knows his children by name.

It's not bad luck that determines your life.

It's not a generational curse that determines your life.

It's not karma, or fate, or the evil eye, or angry saints, that determine your life.

You can't even say the devil made me do it.

No.

Your life sits in the hands of your gracious Heavenly Father, who loves you, and opens doors of opportunity and grace that no one can shut. He empowers you every day to walk through those doors. Your Creator has made you free.

What are you waiting for?

*GENETIC DETERMINISM. I only do what I am genetically programmed to do.*

Why do sharks attack? Sharks attack because that is what they are genetically programmed to do, and too bad for Dory.

A criminal pulls the trigger because that is what a criminal is programmed to do. An abuser raises his fist because that is what an abuser is programmed to do.

Or you can flip it over.

A hero isn't a hero by choice.

People who do what is good and right—that's not a choice either. It's all determined by the genetic cards they were dealt at conception.

*FAMILY TREE DETERMINISM. "My grandpa was a drunk, my dad was a drunk, I'll be a drunk, and my kid will be a drunk."*

> The son shall not bear the guilt of the father, nor the father bear the guilt of the son. The righteousness of the righteous shall be upon himself, and the wickedness of the wicked shall be upon himself. (Ezekiel 18:20)

Your family tree does not define you. That is an illusion.

You may have come from a long line of criminals, addicts, and evil doers. You get to uproot that family tree and plant a new one.

If you come from a really messed up family tree, I have a suggestion for you. Spend some time in prayer, and tell God that you believe that you are not the same as those people.

Claim this scripture as your own:

> For if by the one man's offense death reigned through the one, much more those who receive abundance of grace and of the gift of righteousness will reign in life through the One, Jesus Christ. (Romans 5:17)

I have received the gift of righteousness.

I have received the abundance of grace.

I therefore reign in life, through Jesus Christ, my king.

By the grace of God I will overcome!

I promise you, that if your father or if your mother were in their right mind for even a second, they would look you in the eye and say, "I'm proud of you."

And even if that never happens, when you take your power back, when you reject the determinism of the world, when you look to heaven and say that Christ has redeemed you and you're free, you should know your Father in heaven is more proud of you than you realize.

*SOCIAL DETERMINISM. I am defined by my caste, tribe, group, or economic status, and I can't ever change it.*

Jesus Christ didn't die on the Cross to leave you where he found you.

Determinism offers no reason to resist evil. No reason to pursue justice. It's all determined... why fight it? Why fight anything? Just Zen out, and go with the flow.

If you're born low caste, or low class, just accept it.

Jesus shouted a resounding NO to the social determinism of his day. He embraced lepers. He loved the outcasts. He forgave sinners. His disciples taught...

> There is neither Jew nor Greek, there is neither slave nor free, there is neither male nor female; for you are all one in Christ Jesus. (Galatians 3:28)

They may imprison the body of a child of God, but you don't have to let them imprison your spirit.

*THEOLOGICAL DETERMINISM. God decides everything that happens, and even our choices have been pre-decided by him.*

The word theological simply means having to do with the study of God.

This one is tricky, because we do believe that God is sovereign. He is the caring and powerful ruler of our lives and our world. God sits on the throne of the cosmos. He rules. He reigns. He does his will. He does that which pleases him. No one can defy him and make it stick.

His sovereignty is infinite. His sovereignty is perfect. His sovereignty is glorious. God's will remains supreme.

Now, there are some theological systems that say God is so sovereign that humans have no free will. Or if we do have free will, every decision was pre-ordained by God. Under this view, free will is just an illusion, and God is the ultimate actor in everything.

But, once again, Scripture is clear God has made us free. He has deposited in every heart a measure of his own sovereignty — we have real power to make real choices with real consequences.

> To him who overcomes I will grant to sit with Me on My throne, as I also overcame and sat down with My Father on His throne. (Revelation 3:21)

The sovereign God sits in power on his throne, but notice who else sits there too. The one who overcomes. Who is that? It is you if you grow mature enough as a Christian to use the power that has been given you.

This verse is affirming the infinite sovereignty of God, AND at the same time, teaching the finite sovereignty of the child of God.

You have the same thing again in Romans 5:17: certain people "reign in life" through Jesus.

Who?

"Those who have received the abundance of grace..." Who's that? Every single Christian.

And "those who have received the gift of righteousness..." Who's that? Every single Christian.

*Every single Christian is designed by God to reign in life.*

You sit on the throne of your life. You are spiritual royalty. That means your decisions stick. They are not predetermined by God. You are not stuck on predestinated train tracks.

You have freedom. You have authority. You have the power to choose your course.

It's not train tracks, it's a wide open field and you have a heavenly dirt bike. Go tear it up.

You are created in the image of God. When he made you, he put a few drops of sovereignty into the recipe.

God is sovereign. By his grace, you are a mini-sovereign.

You are not his puppet, and he is not pulling your strings. That is an illusion. Don't fall for it. Reject it.

And the day you stop saying, God made me do it, and I can't help myself, and the devil made me do it... and the day you start saying, "I can do all things through Christ who gives me strength," that is the day the shackles of determinism crumble into a million pieces into so much dust around your feet.

## WHAT CAN WE SAY TO DETERMINISTS?

*1. I agree that we all have some things that we cannot change, but the most important things about me lie within my power to change.*

I can't change where I was born. I can't change the family I was born into. I can't change my genetic code. I can't change my history.

Yes, there are a whole lot of unchangeables in my life.

Maturity means that you accept the unchangeables with dignity and grace, and move on with your life to change what can be changed.

You are not a molecular machine.

You are a body, soul, and spirit, created with a divine spark, and destined for the glories of heaven.

You can rise above the dysfunction of your past. Yes, your family may have given you a shove in a horrible direction, but by the grace of God you can turn around, and change directions.

You can rise above your heartbreaks. You can rise above your losses. You can rise above your habits. You can rise above your addictions. You can rise above your lusts. You can rise above your depression. You can rise above your bitterness. You can rise above your anger. You can rise above your labels. You can rise above your lies.

You can kick the devil in the teeth, take back

your life, and rise to your breathtaking potential as a child of God.

> Yet in all these things we are more than conquerors through Him who loved us. (Romans 8:37)

I can't control everything, but the things I can control, I will control, and by God's grace, I will overcome.

---

*2. I agree that circumstances have power over our lives, but they never become an excuse to remain in defeat.*

Determinism is a philosophy of excuses. It implies you can't be blamed for anything you do. It offers a built-in excuse for every stupid choice: I couldn't help myself.

Determinism always leads to fatalism, and fatalism is always the little voice in your head that whispers, *I am a victim. I am a victim. I am a victim.*

The determinist says, "Judges shouldn't be so quick to send criminals to jail, because criminal behavior is genetically controlled. He can't help that he was born with a criminal gene. It's determined."

I would say, "Well then it's determined that a judge would send the criminal to jail. They can't help themselves either."

The first nobility of the human spirit is that you rise above your animal instincts. You control them. You harness them for good.

The second nobility of the human spirit is that you rule and reign in your life under the mighty Lordship of Jesus Christ.

The third nobility of the human spirit is to take one hundred percent responsibility for the quality of your life under grace.

No excuses. No quitting. No whining. No feeling sorry for yourself.

The wide open promised land of God's blessing and grace stretches to the horizon before you. It belongs to you. God says, go up and take it. Possess your possessions. Be the person you were meant to be. Rise up. Be free.

---

*3. I agree that a complex sequence of events led you to this conversation, so why not declare your faith in Jesus and see what happens?*

Why not?

If salvation isn't "determined," it's not going to stick anyway, so why not give Jesus a try?

There's nothing to lose and everything to gain.

If you're right about determinism, then you hearing these words today is determined. And your response to them is determined. And your faith in

Christ is determined... so why would you resist him today?

The choice is yours:

And the Spirit and the bride say, "Come!" And let him who hears say, "Come!" And let him who thirsts come. Whoever desires, let him take the water of life freely. (Revelation 22:17)

# WORLDLINESS

The premise of this book is both simple and scary: *The ideas that most people believe, shouldn't be believed.*

Let's let that sink in.

Lies run the world. Fake news. Fake truth. Unreality. Deadly philosophy. Spin.

When truth is corrupted, morals are perverted. Because of that, the morals that most people take for granted simply aren't correct either.

People are ensnared *en masse* by the devil's lies. I know this sounds pessimistic, but it is manifestly true.

Perhaps the biggest lie of all says we can have a good world — a just and fair society — without the intervention of the Lord Jesus Christ. It is the lie of Utopia.

*Corrupted creatures cannot create uncorrupted cultures.*

It is impossible.

That is why the main philosophies that drive much of our culture are illusions. Western societies have swallowed the pill that says humans, by human effort, can have a great time without any reference to the God who made them.

This poisonous pill is called *worldliness*. Worldliness is probably not what you think. God's warnings against worldliness echo throughout His Word.

Adulterers and adulteresses! Do you not know that friendship with the world is enmity with God? Whoever therefore wants to be a friend of the world makes himself an enemy of God. (James 4:4)

Do not love the world or the things in the world. If anyone loves the world, the love of the Father is not in him. For all that is in the world--the lust of the flesh, the lust of the eyes, and the pride of life--is not of the Father but is of the world. And the world is passing away, and the lust of it; but he who does the will of God abides forever. (1 John 2:15-17)

There are a whole lot of Bible verses that say

pretty much the same thing. Whatever is meant by *the world*, offers up an alluring illusion. God, who loves you, works overtime to warn you not to get sucked into its heartbreaking house of mirrors.

## WHAT IS WORLDLINESS?

When I was growing up in church, I was taught a radically different definition of worldliness than the one I believe today. Back then, I was taught that worldliness equated with being modern or being up to date.

Rock music was worldly.

Women wearing makeup was worldly.

A woman in my church wore a pantsuit to church, and somebody criticized her for being worldly by not wearing a dress.

Dancing was worldly. Which is why I still have no rhythm.

Playing poker or any card-game was worldly (except Uno). Going to movies. Beer and wine were worldly. Long hair for guys. Short hair for gals. Worldly, worldly, worldly.

If you ever saw the original movie *Footloose*, that was pretty much the history of my life.

Anything that Christians wanted to wag the finger of shame at was labelled as worldly, and shoved into the abyss of God's displeasure.

This made Christians very weird and very

isolated. Our level of holiness was measured by how out of sync we were with society. Somewhere on the spectrum between the Amish and Happy Days.

But the more I studied the Bible, the more I realized that worldliness was something radically different. Let's work our way toward a definition.

The biblical word translated "world" is *kosmos*. *Kosmos,* in this context, doesn't mean the birds in the air or the clouds in the sky or the third planet hurtling around the sun. *Kosmos* means the arrangements, the philosophies, the beliefs, and the worldview of a society, especially as that society is overrun by illusions and lies.

Some experts translate *kosmos* as "world-system" because it captures the idea well. So James warns that friendship with the world-system is hostility with God. John warns that if anyone loves the world-system, the love of the Father is not in them.

We're working our way to a definition of worldliness, so stay with me.

To really define worldliness, we have to add one more element. According to the Bible, the driving force of worldliness is the devil himself.

We know that we are of God, and the whole [world-system] lies under the sway of the wicked one. (1 John 5:19)

The whole world-system is DUI—driving under the influence of Satan.

The devil spewed his acid spit on everything. Morals. Philosophies. Sexuality. Culture. Society. Government.

There's an incredible event in the Bible when the devil tempted Jesus. Three times, our Lord—weakened, tired, and hungry—faced the toughest temptations the devil could launch.

> Then the devil, taking Him up on a high mountain, showed Him all the kingdoms of the world [world-system] in a moment of time. And the devil said to Him, "All this authority I will give You, and their glory; for this has been delivered to me, and I give it to whomever I wish. "Therefore, if You will worship before me, all will be Yours." (Luke 4:5-7)

This was a real temptation. The devil said, "this has been delivered to me." What had been delivered to him? The power over the world-system.

When God created the world, he made it beautiful, and sinless, and good.

He created humans as the pinnacle of creation, and made us in his own image. Then he gave Adam and Eve the scepter of the world. But the devil came and tempted Eve, and Eve tempted Adam, and Adam surrendered the scepter of planet earth to the devil. All these things—the kingdoms of the world and their glory—have been delivered to the devil.

Do not rush by this, and do not take it lightly.

The whole world-system lies under the sway of the wicked one.

- Jesus called the devil "the Ruler of this World-System" (John 12:31).
- Paul called the devil the "God of this Age" (2 Corinthians 4:4).
- John says that the devil deceives the "whole world" (Revelation 12:9).

And here is the biggest problem of all: the devil's influence is subtle. He lurks in the background of his lies, and people who fall for them don't even know he's there.

- And no wonder! For Satan himself transforms himself into an angel of light. (2 Corinthians 11:14)
- "Beware of false prophets, who come to you in sheep's clothing, but inwardly they are ravenous wolves." (Matthew 7:15)
- Be sober, be vigilant; because your adversary the devil walks about like a roaring lion, seeking whom he may devour. (1 Peter 5:8)

Worldly people are not bad people; they are deceived people. They are confused people. They are men and women and students who have been seduced by the dark side, and don't even know it happened.

Except for one really huge clue: *living by worldly philosophy is frustrating and pointless, and ends in a frantic search for a happiness that is always out of reach.*

That's a sign to check your core beliefs, because maybe you've been swallowed by the roaring lion.

What is worldliness?

*Worldliness is unwitting allegiance to philosophies, values, morals, and opinions that have been poisoned by the spit of satanic delusions and therefore draw our hearts away from God.*

Worldliness a beautiful lie — an alternative to God's truth, and a substitute for the blessing of God. It always drags your soul down to a second-rate existence.

Worldliness is spiritual drunk-driving. It is a soul in revolt against God and his truth, wittingly or unwittingly.

You cannot embrace worldliness and love God at the same time, because those are mutually contradictory forces.

Just to make it more crazy, *everything* around you

preaches the gospel of worldliness all the time. You can't escape it, not by accident, at least.

We're talking about Illusions. About Escaping the Matrix, waking up from the dream, shaking off the Zombie state and becoming fully alive in the will and ways of God.

Let's wake up to worldliness.

## WHAT ARE SOME FEATURES OF WORLDLINESS?

*1. HEARTBREAKING. Worldliness as a way of life is a heartbreak waiting to happen.*

What is truth? Truth is reality.

What is truth? Truth is reality as God sees it, God experiences it, God reveals it, and God defines it.

When you align your life with God's truth, everything works right.

- When you align your sexuality with God's truth...
- When you align your relationships, and marriage, and dating, and friendships with God's truth...
- When you align your sources of comfort with God's truth...
- When you align your finances with God's truth...
- When you align your morality with God's truth...

That's when your heart feels satisfied and healthy and whole. Jesus said he came so you could have an abundant, full, radiant, joyful, overflowing life (John 10:10).

But when you fight against God's truth, that's when you're headed for a breakdown. No one can break God's truth. You can only break yourself against God's truth. And worldliness is a way of battering your heart over and over again against the rock of reality.

You may gain the world, but you'll lose your soul. Worldliness is a heartbreak waiting to happen. It is heartbreaking.

---

2. NORMAL. *What the Bible brands as worldliness, the world calls normal.*

If you're not a little weird, you're doing your Christianity wrong.

By weird, I don't mean unstable. I don't mean judgmental. I don't mean off-putting.

By weird, I mean different in ways that make lost people take notice.

I am reading a biography of Mrs. Oswald Chambers ("Biddy"). Some of you know the devotional book she wrote after her husband died, called *My Utmost For His Highest*. Her biography tells a beautiful story of godly weirdness.

Back in the 1800s in England, Biddy Chambers, and her husband Oswald, ran a small Bible college. The cook and the cook's husband were stealing food, and silver, and anything they could purloin, little by little, from the school. The students caught on first. They told Mr. and Mrs. Chambers.

Mr. and Mrs. Chambers decided to wait and to pray. They didn't say anything. All the food that was stolen, Mrs. Chambers replaced with her own money. The chef and the cook started noticing this, but still kept on stealing anyway.

Every time a student pointed out the theft, the Chambers just told them to pray.

After a couple of weeks, the chef and the cook came to Mr. and Mrs. Chambers. They were deeply apologetic and ashamed. They confessed their guilt and said they were sure nobody knew of their crimes. Mr. Chambers said, "Oh, we knew. We knew you were doing it from the start. But we wanted it to be God who pointed it out to you."

Now that is weird. But it is beautifully weird. And that chef and her husband became Christians.

What the world calls weird, God calls normal. What the world calls normal, the God calls worldly.

Normal isn't normal.

Think of what's considered normal today. Sexual expression outside of marriage. Entitlement mentality. Taking from others as a way of life. Living by the sweat of another person's brow.

Protesting. Violence. Disrespect. Diminishing the sacredness of life in any form. Cheating. Cursing. Harassing women. Harassing those who are vulnerable.

The world does not know what normal is, because the world is drunk on the devil's lies.

Dear child of God, don't listen to the world. You have a new normal. Your new normal is finding and following God. Walking where Jesus walked. Thinking God's thoughts after him, and believing a truth that the world can't even begin to see.

> Don't let the world around you squeeze you into its mold. (Romans 12:2, Phil.)

---

*3. SUBTLE. Worldliness presents itself as noble, good, and true, and it's hard to spot its lies.*

American money is basically green and black. If I were printing counterfeit money, what color would I make it? Basically green and black.

Why? Because I want the counterfeit to look as close to the original as possible. That is exactly the devil's plan with worldliness. He doesn't want to be *unlike* God. He wants to be *like* God (Isaiah 14:14).

We could state the devil's agenda this way: His primary agenda is to DISPLACE God and to REPLACE God, and do it in ways that are so subtle we don't realize it's happening. He flies beneath the radar.

The devil's message sounds a lot like God's message, but there is no Jesus, no Cross of Christ, no sin that we need saving from, no salvation through faith alone in Christ alone, and no Bible but what the corrupt heart imagines.

Worldliness is religious, but without the Jesus of Scripture. Worldliness is good, but without the presence of God in the world. The devil is dedicated to a good world. If he had the power, he would eliminate crime. He would eliminate poverty. He would eliminate war. The devil wants to be like Christ. A counterfeit Christ. As close to the real thing as he can be.

This makes it enormously difficult to spot his lies. His untruths sound true. They sound biblical.

At a time when you should be teaching others, you need teachers yourselves to repeat to you the ABC of God's revelation to men. You have become people who need a milk diet and cannot face solid food! For anyone who continues to live on "milk" is unable to digest what is right--he simply has not grown up. "Solid food" is only for the adult, that is, for the man who has developed by experience his power to discriminate between what is good and what is evil. (Hebrews 5:12-14, Phil.)

Worldliness offers a counterfeit grace: it is grace without the cross of Christ and his shed blood.

Worldliness offers a counterfeit gospel: it is making the world a better place, and being kind.

Worldliness offers a counterfeit Jesus: he is a good moral teacher who wasn't virgin born, didn't die for sins, didn't rise from the dead, and isn't coming again, except in some fuzzy, spiritual way to make us all nice.

Worldliness offers a counterfeit morality: never judge anybody except the person who judges anybody.

The reasons illusions exist is because there is a battle going on. It is a battle for your mind. At its deepest level, it is waged by the devil. He longs to drag you away from God. At its everyday level, the devil's lies are often passed on by well meaning, but very confused, people. People who have believed a lie. People who have been sucked into what the Bible calls "strong delusion."

There is a battle for your mind. But it's not always in your face. It is underground. It is subtle. Sly. Sneaky. A battle of gentle persuasion. Seemingly innocent questions. Innocuous insinuations. Seducing you to the dark side, and you don't even know it's happening.

We need critical thinking because the world is so sneaky.

But we can't have critical thinking God's way

unless we are loaded up with Scripture. It's not about human IQ, it's about spiritual IQ. God's truth, God's theology, God's doctrines, God's teachings, God's promises, God's commands, God's heart, all hardwired into your own heart from God's inerrant Word.

---

4. *DEFINING STORY. Worldliness offers a box-top picture to put together the disconnected pieces of your life and your world, but the pieces don't fit.*

We all acquire our truth in bits and pieces. A little here, a little there. We get snippets of truth at different times, in different places, from different teachers, and experiences.

They are like pieces of a gigantic puzzle.

There's a deep drive inside the human heart to put all those pieces together. This is the only way we can make sense of our lives and our world.

Worldliness offers a box-top picture to put those pieces together. It is this box-top picture that is the devil's primary weapon in the battle for your mind.

The battle is a fight over stories. Defining stories. Big stories. Cultural myths. Or, to use the annoying language of philosophy, it is a battle of meta-narratives. A meta-narrative is the story about the story. It is a giant, pre-packaged story that contains the story of your life and your world. You're part of a much bigger story. It is a structured story. It is made of many parts, and the parts fit together like pieces of a puzzle.

*Here is the secular atheist story:*

The cosmos is all that is or was or ever will be. Once upon a time, a singularity exploded, and everything came into existence. There is the realm of matter and energy, and nothing above it. Everything is the interaction of matter and energy. There is no god, no eternity, no afterlife, no prayer, no rational faith, no angels, no devil, no heaven, and no hell. All life is the product of random chance — chemical ping pong balls bouncing in an energy soup.

This is the story being aggressively pushed in top universities, media, politics, science, and government.

This story is the foundation of worldliness. It serves up its own religion: All is one and all is god and god is in you and you are in god, and you are god. All things merge into one cosmic consciousness in the end.

This is the story being aggressively pushed in media, entertainment, social sciences, and the arts.

I'm saying that the worldly philosophy is a package deal. It is one giant story. The only sin is to question the story you're being told. To resist it and push back against the story. Resistance makes you dangerous.

Do not be fooled.

The world is vicious about protecting its story. It wants no competitors. Because once the world erased the supremacy of God, something had to take the place of God. Something has to be supreme. That something has become the story and the people who tell it.

It's all a bunch of lies.

They have deified themselves. They have deified their narrative.

And their wrath rains down on anyone who pushes back against them.

Perhaps the saddest part is that every worldly narrative always breaks your heart.

> Beware lest anyone cheat you through philosophy and empty deceit, according to the tradition of men, according to the basic principles of the [world-system], and not according to Christ. (Colossians 2:8)

There is a battle for your mind, which is to say, there is a battle over which story of the universe you will believe. And as long as you go along with the collective, you will be popular and rewarded.

But the moment you call out the lies, you are branded as dangerous. Nothing will stop them from tearing you apart. You are in a war. Aren't you glad you picked up this book?

There is good news.

It is a WINNABLE war.

Because we have a defining story that is the most beautiful, life-affirming, transcendent story ever told. It begins with "In the Beginning, God created the heavens and the earth" and ends with a new heaven and new earth with no more sorrow or tears.

In between stands the Cross of Christ, triumphing over the brokenness of humankind.

The very moment you get *that* big story programmed into your soul, you will rise in victory for the first time over the philosophies of the world, you will stand as a champion of grace, and you will experience the love of God in your heart like you have never known it before.


## HOW TO AVOID THE TRAPS OF WORLDLINESS

How do we avoid the traps of worldliness?

By consistent progress along the Grace Pathway.

The Bible isn't a million things. It's one simple, clear, patterned way of life.

1. God saves you.
2. God blesses you.
3. God grows you.
4. God uses you.

If you get on that pathway, you will become a

walking, talking, living, breathing miracle called "the God-blessed life."

> For the weapons of our warfare are not carnal but mighty in God for pulling down strongholds, casting down arguments and every high thing that exalts itself against the knowledge of God, bringing every thought into captivity to the obedience of Christ. (2 Corinthians 10:4,5)

A previous generation of Christians didn't talk much about discipleship—a word that never occurs in the epistles. They largely used the term *spiritual maturity*. It's a far more helpful term—more clear, more focused, and less legalistically tainted.

The way to escape the dream-state is to grow in grace. The way to uproot worldliness is to grow toward maturity. The way to escape the matrix of illusions and worldliness, and the way to take your stand on the sunny highlands of God's amazing grace, is by growing up in the Lord.

What is worldliness?

Worldliness is a person joining the devil's temper tantrum against the Heavenly Father.

So, I gently say, to the people of God, in Christian love, *Stop kicking and screaming and quit being such a baby.*

Christian, grow up.

## POPULARITY

The year was 1885. In one city alone, 90,000 people died needlessly. That city was my hometown, Chicago. The reason so many people died that year was horrible and simple at the same time: they died because they drank the water.

Chicago sits alongside Lake Michigan. It seems as big as an ocean, but it's fresh water. The city draws its drinking water from the Lake.

But back then, there was a problem with the Lake. The Chicago River flowed into Lake Michigan.

And that is why so many people died in 1885. The businesses and industries of Chicago were dumping their waste into the Chicago River. The sewage of three quarters of a million people was flushed into the Chicago River. And since the Chicago River flowed into Lake Michigan, and since Lake Michigan provided drinking water for the city, a huge outbreak of disease happened that year. Outbreaks of Typhoid, Cholera, and Dysentery diseases killed twelve percent of the city's population in the year 1885.

So the city came up with a solution. The solution was one of the most ambitious projects ever since the Pharaohs built the pyramids. Using only the technology of the 1800s, the City of Chicago reversed the flow of the Chicago River.

There's never been anything like it.

They dug canals. They built locks. They blasted through 12 million cubic yards of solid rock. They pushed away 26 million yards of dirt. They dug a new river bed. It was the most massive earth moving project in human history. It took 15 years. It cost $70 million, a huge expense for the day. And it employed a staggering army of workers to get it done.

But on January 2, 1900, the locks were opened, and for the first time in geologic history, water flowed out of Lake Michigan, into the Chicago River, to the Illinois River, to the Mississippi River, all the way to New Orleans.

They reversed a river.

It was declared the "Civil Engineering Achievement of the Millennium" in 1999.

I say this, because God needs to do some massive work in order to reverse the flow of much of our thinking.

Don't let the world around you squeeze you into its own mold, but let God re-make you so that your whole attitude of mind is changed. Thus you will prove in practice that the will of God is good, acceptable to him and perfect. (Romans 12:2, Phil.)

## AGAINST THE CURRENT

Every single time you walk out of your house, and into your job, your school, your neighborhood, or Youtube, Instagram, Snapchat, Social media... If you interact with the world in any way at all, you will immediately be pushed along by the current of society.

The hard part is that you're moving, and might not even know it.

Right now, the surface of the earth is spinning at about 1,000 miles per hour compared to the core.

Right now, the planet earth is racing at 67,000 miles per hour compared to the sun.

The only reason you don't feel the speed is because you're moving at the exact same speed as everything around you.

The current around you has become the current within you.

I wrote this book to help reverse the current within you. The current of prevailing philosophies.

The current of misguided beliefs. Those philosophies are illusions, and they will break your heart.

So God lovingly says, Don't let the world around
you squeeze you into its mold. Don't flow with that
current.

Turn around.

This is much more easily said than done.


## POPULARITY

I was always the most popular kid in school. Everybody wanted to be my friend, and everybody
thought I was awesome. The reason is probably
because you just can't contain all this coolness.*
(*Actually, I was kind of a nerd.)

I was always on the cutting edge of fashion.*
(*Actually, my brother makes fun of me for never
wearing blue jeans in high school because they
weren't classy enough.)

I was also a member of the very hip chess club.

Even better, I was a member of the extremely
exclusive Latin Club.* (*I may or may not have worn
a toga.)

And always a trend-setter with hair styles.* (*Re-
sults may vary.)

Okay, so maybe I wasn't as cool or as popular as I
remember. Actually, I wasn't that cool at all. I didn't
play any sports in school. I wasn't in any bands. I
didn't have a girlfriend in high school. And I didn't

go to my proms. My church was against proms, and to be honest, I was kind of relieved. Too much pressure.

Plus I'm an introvert, and God loves introverts best.

Popularity isn't a bad thing. And it's not necessarily a good thing.

It's just not the most important thing. That everybody likes you or knows you or thinks you are cool.

How much do you think Jesus cared about popularity?

Study after study shows the same thing: that being popular in high school and college does not equate to being successful in marriage, in business, in money, or in life.

There's a reason why: because there is something about a thousand times more important than popularity.

And that is *character*.

When you make the shift from *popularity* to *character* as a motivating force, you are swimming upstream, breaking the mold, and reversing the course of your life's river.

Let's break the illusion of popularity.

Let's take our stand on the rock-solid reality of character.

Here are some reasons why character beats popularity.

## WHY CHARACTER > POPULARITY

*1. Because popularity wears masks, but character reveals the heart.*

In the ancient world, people went to massive theatrical productions. These were held in outside amphitheaters. There was no lighting really, and no iMag. To help theater-goers back in the cheap seats, the actors wore masks. They were big, exaggerated emoji's, basically. Smiley faces. Frowny faces. Angry faces. They wore masks.

Those masks had a name.

In the Greek language, they were called "*hypokrites*" [pronounced hu-POK-rit-tace].

This is the origin of our English word *hypocrite*. A hypocrite is a person who wears a mask. They manifest a false face.

Why would somebody do that?

When I was in high school, I read a book that really hit me hard. It was called *Why Am I Afraid To Tell You Who I Am* (John Powell, Zondervan, 1969).

Here was the big idea: "I am afraid to tell you who I am because if I tell you who I am, you may not like who I am, and that is all I have."

People who value popularity more than character are always showing you only what they want you to see. Popularity buries a person's identity under ever changing masks. It's not about being myself, it's about portraying whatever manufactured self I think other people will accept.

In contrast, character drops the masks. Character presents the best version of my true self, satisfied that God loves me, even if I never win any popularity contests. Character expresses self-respect coupled with a realistic view of my faults. When character guides me, I'm free from the tyranny of other people's opinions. That's because I've already won the most important prize of all: the perfect acceptance of God, now and forevermore. That's good enough for me.

Here's a second reason why character is greater than popularity.

---

*2. Because popularity uses people, but character uplifts people.*

If popularity is my top priority, when I look at you, I have one question in mind: *what can you do for me?*

Does that sound like how Jesus treated people?

There's a really interesting verse in the Bible that a lot of people get wrong. It's from the Bible's famous Love Chapter, which is 1 Corinthians 13. You might have heard part of this chapter read at weddings.

Here's the cryptic verse in the middle of the chapter.

> For now we see in a mirror, dimly, but then face
> to face. Now I know in part, but then I shall know
> just as I also am known. (1 Corinthians 13:12)

This verse is talking about Love.

It is especially talking about the kind of love that you can have when you become a mature, grown up, spiritually mature Christian.

Interpreters have wrestled for years over the meaning of the mirror in this verse. Most of them say this verse is talking about heaven. As long as we're stuck on earth, life feels like looking in a dull mirror. Everything is dim and confusing. But one day, in heaven, we'll see Jesus clearly, face to face. No more distortions.

That is a lovely sentiment, and it is one hundred percent true. Unfortunately, it is not anywhere close to what this verse is talking about. It is an incorrect, though painfully common, interpretation.

This verse is talking about *love*, not *heaven*. The character quality called love is front and center. Let's allow the context to guide our interpretation. Think about a couple of questions.

*Question 1*: when you are looking in a mirror, who are you looking at?

*Answer 1*: you're looking at yourself. Am I hot or not? Did I make a good impression? What are people thinking of me? Am I better than the other person? I. Me. My.

When your character revolves around yourself, the beautiful quality of love is buried in an avalanche of narcissism.

First Corinthians 13:12 says, "For now, we see in a mirror dimly..." By now, he means, "in a state of spiritual immaturity." This is that time in any person's life when popularity is more important than character. A spiritual child. Narcissism gobbles up love faster than a teenage breakup.

Not only that, it makes life confusing. That's what the word "dimly" means in this verse. It is the Greek word, *ainigma.* Scripture is warning that, in a state of immaturity, a person is focused so on themselves, that life feels like a giant enigma. Why? Because they are trapped in illusions.

Finally, the verse shifts focus. "But then..."

When?

When a person has grown mature enough to have shed the illusions of popularity, and to have grown mature in character and love,.

"But then, face to face."

*Question 2*: When you are looking "face to face," who are you looking at?

*Answer 2*: You are looking at the other person instead of yourself. That is love. And love requires character.

Will you be kind to people who can't do anything for you?

Will you reach out to people who sit alone at lunch and invite them to join you?

When you are in a circle of friends, will you open the circle, and call over someone who isn't part of your little clique?

That is the type of "face to face" love Jesus showed. It is the type of love he wants to produce in you. Character-driven love. Character uplifts people. Popularity exploits people.

Character looks into the eyes of other people as windows to their soul. Character is generous without resentment and sacrificial without regret. When you develop character, you can give of yourself without losing yourself.

The world desperately needs this mature, truly loving, character. Developing it requires swimming upstream. Are you willing to do that?

Another reason why character is so much more valuable than popularity is this:

---

3. *Because popularity is slavery, but character is freedom.*

Go back to the masks people wear. I have an acquaintance, who looks like a different person every time I see him. He's a melancholy guy anyway. But he's always giving himself total makeovers. I know that some people do that out of strength.

But I think he's doing it out of weakness. I think

he's desperately searching for an identity that other people will like.

So he tries on this mask... how do you like me now?

And then the next mask... hot or not?

And then the next mask... do you like this look?

He has tried so many identities I don't think he knows who he really is.

The day you enter a popularity contest with your peers is the day you surrender control of your SELF to the opinion of others.

That isn't freedom, it's slavery.

Character is different. Character says, "This is me. I am who God says I am. I am not who the bullies say I am. I am not who the mean girls say I am. I am not who my absent, dysfunctional, stoned, selfish, parents or guardians say I am.

"I am saved. God has joined me to Christ. I am who God says I am."

When I was a freshman in high school, my English teacher told us to write a paper called, *Who Am I?*

I was only fourteen at the time. At that age, I don't know who I am. I don't have the slightest clue. So I start typing away. "I am Bill. I am Italian. I am..." and I ran out of stuff to say.

That night, I went to church for Prayer Meeting. I passed a lady in the hall, and she asked me, "Hey Bill, why do you look so miserable?"

First I adjusted my face. Then I told her about this stupid paper I had to write. "Who Am I?"

She said, "Oh, that's easy. I am a child of God. I am a citizen of heaven. I am spiritual royalty... a member of the household of faith."

In that moment, fourteen years of Sunday School clicked with me. I get it! I'm a Christian! That's the main thing! When I got home, I wrote my paper, no problem.

I am who God says I am. As long I base my character on that truth, all the illusions melt away.

When God looks at me, he sees Bill plus Christ. As Jesus is to God, so am I.

Is Jesus strong? Then I am strong. Is Jesus welcomed? Then I am welcomed. Is he accepted? Then I am accepted. Is he good enough for God? Then so am I.

The moment I let God define me I shed the shackles of other people's opinions.

Character is self-mastery. It is self-control by the power of God's Word and God's Spirit. It is the true royalty and nobility God made you for.

Character is me being me, and you being you, and both of us being good with that.

Character is me dropping the masks, and feeling confident to just be myself. It allows me to accept my truest, deepest self. Through growth in maturity and character, God unburies me from the avalanche of craziness, dysfunction, and sin that has piled over the real me.

It's not everybody's opinion that tells me who I am.

It is the character inside of me knowing that I am linked to Christ, and I am who God says I am no matter what else anybody says. "Don't let the world around you squeeze you into its mold."

I am writing to unleash the real you! The best you! The You you think you can be on days when your faith is strong. It's so rare. It's so against the current.

Dear child of God, be yourself.

A fourth reason why the character operating system beats the popularity OS is this.

---

4. *Because popularity takes the path of least resistance, but character pushes against the current.*

Popularity is flabby.

Character is rock hard. A backbone of steel.

I wasn't ashamed of being a Christian. Everybody knew. I witnessed to my friends. I argued apologetics. I tried to show them Jesus was true.

I went to Lane Tech High School, over 5,000 students strong. A few of us gathered every morning on the steps to pray for our friends to get saved. My brother and I started that.

We didn't care if people thought we were weird. We just did it.

Okay, I did care a little. Actually a lot. I was very self-conscious. I felt like a nerd.

But the character that Christ was forming in me was more important than being popular, or well-liked, or cool.

Every morning, I got up early before school. And I had to take a Chicago Public Transportation bus to and from school — so bus/train/bus, but I got up early to study my Bible, and take notes, and pray.

That stuck with me.

I'm not saying I was perfect, and I'm not bragging.

I was simply very conscious of not letting the world around me squeeze me into its mold, and I knew the only way to do that was through daily Bible study.

That's my prayer for you.

Because you can't reverse the flow within your heart and soul, without the power of the Word of God.

---

5. *Because popularity is natural and human, but character is supernatural from the power of Christ in you, the Spirit in you, and the Word in you.*

I understand the desire to be popular and liked

and well-known. I wrestle with that all the time. But there is something far more important. Character. I know that I haven't defined character, and I want to do that right now.

Character comes from a Greek word that meant "the creator's mark." A "character" was engraved on metals, and carved into wood, or scribed into pottery.

When you have character, God is marking you as his own masterpiece.

What is the mark?

*Character is the divine mark by which God produces in you the same qualities that made Jesus so beautiful, and so powerful, and so different from everybody else.*

Character is the mark of wisdom. The mark of courage. The mark of kindness. The mark of discernment. The mark of self-possession. The mark of joy. The mark of love.

The Spirit, however, produces in human life fruits such as these: love, joy, peace, patience, kindness, generosity, fidelity, tolerance and self-control--and no law exists against any of them. (Galatians 5:22, 23, Phil.)

This is the character of Christ. It is the fruit of the Spirit.

Have you ever seen an apple grow? How does the tree make it?

Does it strain, groan, labor, sweat, and push?

No. It is the fruit—the natural outcome of a healthy life process—of the Spirit, whose power operates every time you open the Bible and believe it.

I would rather be friends with a person who has that kind of character than with the most popular people in the world.

If you are growing in the character of Christ, but you are not popular, the only reason is because the people around you are so locked into their illusions, and so caught in the current of the world, they don't know an awesome person when they see one.

---

## CHARACTER > POPULARITY HONOR CODE

When I first wrote this section, I was thinking mainly of students in high school and college. I'm hoping they will get together and covenant to care for each other. The more I have thought about it, however, the more I realize how much *everybody* needs to go deeper in their friendships.

So I'm proposing that adult small groups as well as student youth groups create their own covenants to elevate *character* above *popularity*, and to make sure that somebody has their backs.

Here's a sample honor code with some commentary:

*1. I will cultivate a friendship (small group) where I can increasingly be honest and open about my struggles and desires.*

Keep it safe. Keep it balanced. Create a bond of friendship.

*2. I will reach out to a person who seems alone, isolated, or sad.*

Not in an arrogant way where I'm their Savior, but in a kind and friendly way.

You need to be kind to each other *at school* and *on the job*. You need to take care of each other. You need to say encouraging words. You need to not be bossy. You need to bless and have each other's backs. You need to stick up for each other.

You're going against a very strong flow every single day, and maybe together you can be the ones to reverse the flow, and uplift an entire institution.

One of the largest churches in America began when a group of high school students in a small church, came together to pray, and encourage each other. And they started sharing and helping each other in really beautiful ways.

*3. I will discover and claim my true identity in Christ.*

The Bible lists about three dozen statements that are true of you. I am blessed. I am beloved. I am redeemed. I am justified. The more you study those, the more your self esteem grows.* (I wrote a book called *Grace Rehab* to help with this.)

*4. I will speak words of grace and truth, even if people think I'm weird.*

Jesus came speaking words of grace and truth, and some people loved him, and some people hated him, but nobody was bored by him.

We should be known by our love. God says you're not the same as everybody else. You go against the flow.

And that means your words. And your relationships with the unpopular people.

I was blown away when I was in high school, and one of my Sunday school teachers said — and it's weird, but stick with me — "What if no matter what somebody said to us, we could reply by quoting a Bible verse, especially the sayings of Jesus?"

So we started a group to memorize big chunks of the Bible. And I did that, in high school. NoI don't go around talking that way, because it would turn people off to Jesus.

But it has impacted me. Speak words of grace and truth, and don't worry about your popularity.

*5. I will grow spiritually, and seek to be mature in Bible study, prayer, and likeness to Christ.*

God saves you, blesses you, grows you, and uses you. This is God's plan for your life. Get with it.

Don't stay a spiritual baby. Get into the Word of God. Get in a Bible study. Grow.

Grow up, grow strong, reverse the current, swim against the flow, and please, don't let the world around you squeeze you into its heartbreaking, society-fracturing, God-insulting, life-wrecking, illusion-infected, people-exploiting mold.

# EVOLUTION

I grew up in two worlds—the world of church, and the world of the Chicago public school system.

In the world of church, I learned that I was created in the image of God.

In the world of the public school system, I learned I evolved from lower forms of life.

My church taught me I was body, soul, and spirit, with a spark of life lit by the breath of God. The universe was God-centered. It was created by him, and existed for his glory. I had an eternal soul and would live forever, either with or without God.

In my church, I learned all creation was infused with the presence of God, and everyday of life was supercharged with transcendent value.

My school told me a different story. I was a matter and energy molecular machine plus nothing.

The universe was an accident, and had no purpose. I was an accident too, bound by time, and when my chemical machine wore out, I snuffed out like a candle, and that was it. There was nothing after death.

In my school, I learned that the space-time continuum was all there is, and every day of life was defined by the survival of the fittest.

The world of church lifted the veil of existence and showed me the face of a Creator God upholding and redeeming all things. I am the epitome of creation.

The world of school showed me a mechanical universe with no soul. I am the product of evolution.

I grew up in both worlds. And all through childhood, these two worlds coexisted inside me peacefully. I was too young, too immature, and to unsophisticated see the contradiction.

In my junior year of high school, something clicked inside me. My two worlds collided. It hit me that both couldn't be right. Either I was the epitome of divine creation from a personal God, or I was the product of random chance in an impersonal cosmos. Both of those couldn't be true.

I was seventeen, and it was my first crisis of faith. The crisis grew strong really fast. You have to understand how much church meant to me. It was my home away from home. My primary relationships were at church. I was loved. I was valued. I was important. Church defined me.

The truths I learned in Sunday school, the verses I learned in Awana, the relationships I formed, the people who were my spiritual fathers and mothers in the faith — that was my heart, my core... church defined me. I couldn't bear to lose it.

Yet there was a war going on inside me. I was interested in science. I had my own microscope because I wanted to be a microbiologist. I loved both worlds, but my mind was racing trying to put it all together. Was I a transcendent creation of almighty God or matter and energy in a chemical soup?

It was a huge struggle for me, but I didn't tell anybody.

One of the most influential people in my life was a Sunday school teacher named Karl. I remember being at his house with a bunch of other youth, and he could tell something was wrong. I was in his kitchen. People were playing Uno and eating pizza. Karl and I were standing by the kitchen counter, hanging out. He could tell I had a struggle.

"Bill," he said. "Is there something wrong?"

I wanted to say, "I can't tell if creation is true or evolution is true, and I'm ready to toss out my faith over this conflict." That's what I wanted to say. But I didn't say it. I said, "Nothing is wrong. I'm all good."

By the second semester of junior year, I was really conflicted.

I knew I had to resolve this conflict. Thankfully, the school offered a way to do that. I had to write a term paper on any topic I wanted. I chose creation and evolution. I gathered every book I could find on the topic, and back then—in the icy age before Internet—there were only a few. I read. I studied. I dug in. It was the first time ever I had heard about scientific support for creation. It blew me away. Yes, it was a function of faith, but it was more than faith. It was also the first time I made another discovery: evolution is science, but it's more than science. It's has a whole lot of faith, too.

I became convinced of creation. I became convinced by studying the facts. And ever since then, as the years have passed, I've only grown more convinced by the facts themselves. And I can stand here today, and testify that everything I needed to know about myself and my world begins with the majestic words: In the beginning, God created the heavens and the earth.

## WHAT IS EVOLUTION?

*1. Evolution is "descent with modification; transformation of species through time, including both changes that occur within species, as well as the origin of new species." (Jonathan Locos, Princeton Univ. Press)*

This simple definition states that evolution is "descent with modification." That was Darwin's definition. A species is modified as it passes down the generations.

The expanded definition, however, is incorrect. Locos includes changes that occur within species, and well as the origin of new species. That is incorrect.

Changes within a species is not evolution. It is, technically, adaptation. All species adapt. Butterflies change the colors of their wings, but they are still the same butterflies with the same genetic code. This has been observed over and over again by scientists.

To be evolution, the change must create a new species, with a new genetic code. This has never been observed by science.

A resource from Berkeley says this:

*The central idea of biological evolution is that all life on earth shares a common ancestor, just as you and your cousins share a common grandmother... Evolution means that we're all distant cousins: humans and oak trees, hummingbirds and whales.*

— UNDERSTANDING EVOLUTION

That's possibly the worst illustration in the history of science. The comparison is completely irrelevant. You are related to your grandmother by *birth*. You are related, under evolution, to other living things by a *theory* of a common life origin—something radically different.

Evolution is the theory that all life descended from a common living organism. Evolution requires that all new species arose through extremely long cycles of random mutation and natural selection.

## FEATURES OF EVOLUTION

*1. THEORY. Evolution is a theory: The Theory of Evolution.*

Theory means it is not a proven fact. It is not an observable fact. It is a hypothesis. Theory means it is one suggested way of putting together all the observable facts.

There is another theory, called CREATION, which takes the same observable facts and puts them together differently.

*CREATION is the theory, revealed in Scripture, that all that is, including life, is created by God, and that humans are made in God's own image.*

The observable facts are: a) the huge diversity of life on planet earth; b) the fossil record.

Science has never observed a new species emerge — not by observation in the present, and not by observation of the past through the fossil record. Science requires observation. Evolution requires the emergence of new species. Since the emergence of new species has never been observed, past or present, technically, evolution can only be called a theory and not a fact. That was the first lesson that blew my mind so long ago. Because there is one thing you have to learn about science: scientists are human too, and therefore can be biased, and political, and self-protected, and blind to their own presuppositions. Hopefully, they account for their biases. Many times, they do not. Evolution remains a theory.

It is not a proven fact.

Here is another key element within the evolutionary theory:

---

2. *RANDOM MUTATION. Random genetic mutation alters the DNA of a species, in a beneficial direction.*

Evolution requires this to happen. It says that a random genetic mutation has to happen.

So, one day, a bird hatches that has a genetic mutation that gave it a longer beak. That mutation happened randomly, by accident. But the nice thing about it, was that it was beneficial to the bird. The longer beak helped the bird eat more bugs. The longer beak helped it fight off snakes. The longer beak was beneficial to the bird... and because the bird had the gene for the longer beak (genetic mutation), it passed on the longer beak to its offspring.

And the next baby hatchling had the same longer beak.

But it has to be favorable. It has to be beneficial. The vast majority of genetic mutations are not favorable. They harm the organism, they don't help it. Evolution can only happen when beneficial mutations happen. If it doesn't help, then the next feature can't kick in. That's important. Say it with me: gradual and beneficial.

---

*3. NATURAL SELECTION. Natural selection is nature's process to gradually lock in beneficial genetic mutations by passing them down to the offspring.*

This is where the famous line comes in: "Survival of the fittest."

> *I have called this principle, by which each slight variation, if useful, is preserved, by the term Natural Selection, in order to mark its relation to man's power of selection. But the expression often used by Mr. Herbert Spencer of the Survival of the Fittest is more accurate, and is sometimes equally convenient.*

> — CHARLES DARWIN, FROM ORIGIN
> OF SPECIES

*4. MATERIALISM. Materialism is the view that every-thing that exists is matter and energy and is totally explainable by science.*

No God, no angels, no heaven, no hell, no prayer. No spirit and no soul.

Until Darwin popularized evolution, it was really hard to hold onto materialism. There was simply no reasonable explanation of our complex minds.

Evolution has given society an excuse to erase the soul, erase eternity, and erase the God who made us all.

But because of evolution, Carl Sagan could now begin his famous book, *The Cosmos*, with the words, "The Cosmos is all that is, and all that ever was, and all that ever will be."

Materialism robs the world of its splendor, humans of their dignity, and life of its meaning.


## WHAT CAN WE SAY TO OUR HIGHLY EVOLVED FRIENDS?

*1. MOTIVE. What is your motive for believing in evolu-tion? Really, why do you believe it?*

Very few people have read the science. Even fewer have read the creationist arguments. So most people are just going with the flow, and they are not curious enough intellectually, or they are too lazy perhaps to really think about where they came from.

But society has latched on to evolution. Society has latched principally because of worldliness. To believe in creation is to believe in a Creator. To believe in a Creator is to make ourselves accountable to him. And people are allergic to accountability.

The Bible says people...

- Exchanged the truth of God for a lie... (Romans 1:25)
- Worshipped the creation rather than the Creator... (Romans 1:25)
- Did not like to retain God in their knowledge... (Romans 1:28)

Picture a person going through the drive through.

"Thanks for stopping, Sinner. Would you like your life with God or without God?"

"Without God, please."

But that immediately creates a problem.

There's a little voice inside called *conscience* where God whispers... *I am here. I am right before your eyes. Look at my fingerprints — they're everywhere. Ask yourself... where did you come from? Where did everything in this world come from?*

There are two questions no human can ever outrun: Where did I come from? Where am I going?

Those were the questions that drove my quest during high school. Mankind's origin. Mankind's destiny.

The world has latched onto evolution mainly

because it permits them to answer those questions without resorting to God. Very few will admit it, but that's the deepest motive, if people were brutally honest.

There's another problem for the theory of evolution.

---

*2. COMPLEXITY. Even the simplest life form is far more complex than evolution can explain.*

In the evolution I learned as I grew up, there was a swamp on earth. Inside the swamp were certain chemicals and molecules. One day a lightning strike mixed up the right chemicals in the right moment, supercharged with the right aligning strike and BAM life emerged.

That life was very simple. It was a single cell life form. It had a cell wall, with a nucleus inside. The rest of the cell was filled with something called protoplasm. As I learned it, protoplasm was a simple clear jelly, and it was alive. It was living goo. And every simple life form was filled with it, with protoplasm.

It was reasonable to believe, because it was so simple. It wasn't complex. Cell wall. Protoplasm. Nucleus. Life had evolved. Easy.

However, that was the age before electron microscopes. Today, scientists know there is nothing simple inside even the simplest cell.

The cell wall is a miracle of complexity itself. It is thinner than a spider's thread, electrically charged, and has pores though which it admits the molecules it needs and expels the molecules it doesn't need.

Inside the cell wall is the complex machinery of the cell. Each living cell is a shrine to God's genius and precision. Lysosomes, endoplasmic reticulum, Golgi apparatus and many more complex structures inhabit the world inside the cell. The mitochondria produce as much electricity as the power lines above your head. The exchange of oxygen and carbon dioxide is a wonder to behold. The ATP created and burned to fuel an athlete is equal to the athlete's body weight every single day. The inside of a cell is a crowded and masterful system of interconnected parts.

The nucleus contains a single strand of DNA. It measures only 50 trillionths of an inch thick. Even though it is smaller than a speck of dust, if you were to stretch out that single strand of DNA, it would be as tall as you are. If you were to stretch out all the DNA in your body end to end, it would go 10 billion (some say up to 170 billion) miles.

There is no such thing as a "simple" life form.

Every piece of every cell of every life is complex beyond human understanding.

When I was growing up, my teachers used this

illustration to teach evolution. They said that if we had enough monkeys typing on enough typewriters (an antique keyboard), they would eventually type out all the writings of Shakespeare, just by random chance. Just give them a whole lot of time, like a 150 billion years.

Every honest scientist today knows this is false.

One scientist at the University of Paris did the math. He concluded, "There is no chance ($<10^{-1000}$) to see this [evolutionary] mechanism appear spontaneously..."

A molecular biophysicist calculated that if one were to take the simplest living cell and break every chemical bond within it, the odds that the cell could reassemble itself would be $10^{-100,000,000,000}$.

Going back to the monkey analogy, one famous mathematician calculated that if you gave those monkeys all the time the universe has been in existence, they would only type one half of a line from one book by accident.

There is not enough matter in the universe to make enough monkeys and enough typewriters to type out even one book by random chance, given all the time the universe is supposed to have existed.

An article in Scientific American, which is pro-evolution, said that the odds of the spontaneous emergence of a single cell organism emerging randomly from a primordial swamp is about as likely as assembling a fully functional Boeing 747 by a tornado whirling through a junkyard. And I would add you still need somebody to fly it.

The math just doesn't work.

Even the simplest life form is a marvel. And that is because it was created from the hand of an all knowing, all powerful, utterly imaginative Creator God. David was right when he said,

> You made all the delicate, inner parts of my body and knit me together in my mother's womb. (Psalm 139:13, NLT)

3. *IRREDUCIBLE COMPLEXITY. How can evolution account for the gradual development of the complex systems in every living form?*

This idea of irreducible complexity was first published in a best selling book by Michale Behe, called *Darwin's Black Box*. I've been reading on creation/evolution for a lot of years, and this was the final nail in evolution's coffin for me.

Irreducible complexity refers to a single system composed of several interacting parts, so that removal of any of the parts makes the system stop functioning.

Let me illustrate it with a mouse trap. It has basically nine parts. Ten, if you count the bait. It's a very simple machine.

If you take away just one of its parts, the mouse trap stops working.

Remember two key words for the evolutionary theory: *gradual* and *beneficial*. That's how natural selection works. It locks in *gradual* and *beneficial* chance mutations. No *gradual* and *beneficial*, no natural selection. No natural selection, no evolution.

Go back to the mouse trap. There is no way it came together gradually. Because part 1 by itself offered no benefit, so natural selection wouldn't lock it in. Parts 1 and 2 together offer no benefit, so natural selection wouldn't lock 1 and 2 in. Parts 1, 2, and 3 offer no benefit, and so on and so on. This machine could not be assembled by small incremental steps, because it is nonfunctional till all the parts are present at once.

The whole thing had to be put together at once for it to be beneficial. Gradual wouldn't work.

Charles Darwin himself stated:

*"If it could be demonstrated that any complex organ existed which could not possibly have been formed by numerous, successive, slight modifications, my theory would absolutely break down."*

— ORIGIN OF THE SPECIES

Now, let's go to a simple living organism like bacteria.

You might remember from freshman biology that some of these bacteria swim around with a tail, called a flagellum.

What you might not know is that a flagellum is an incredibly complex molecular machine. It is a tiny outboard motor. The flagellum spins anywhere from 6,000 up to 100,000 revolutions per minute. It can reverse in an instant. Scientists say it operates at 97% energy efficiency. This little living machine is a marvel of engineering.

The flagellum has between 30 and 40 working parts, so it is quite complex.

Now here's the important thing: Take away even one working part, and the whole motor stops functioning. This is the meaning of Behe's term, "irreducible complexity." You can't take away even one part or it won't work.

So here is the giant middle linebacker to tackle the theory of evolution.

How did 30 to 40 parts come together *gradually* when there was no benefit until all thirty parts showed up at once, all put together?

Remember the two words, *gradual* and *beneficial*? They can't apply here.

To belabor the point, recall Darwin's statement: "If it could be demonstrated that any complex organ existed which could not possibly have been formed by numerous, successive, slight modifications, my theory would absolutely break down." (Origin of the Species)

Well here you go, Mr. Darwin. Have a flagellum. Parts 1 through 5 might show up, but the flagellum wouldn't spin. Parts 6 through 10 might appear together in a soup, but the flagellum wouldn't spin. Parts 11 through — well, you get the idea. Since there is no *benefit*, there can be no evolution, no natural selection, no incremental modification.

It is impossible, and evolution has no explanation for these complex, miniature sub-structures of life.

Since natural selection cannot explain the step-by-step assembly of complex cellular machines, the whole theory of evolution falls apart. But it gets worse for evolution.

Not only is the machine itself irreducibly complex.

The assembly process is also irreducibly complex. If I put all the parts of a simple mousetrap in a bag and shook it up, it still wouldn't produce a mousetrap. Or a car. or an eyeball. Or a brain. Shaking won't do it. Random bouncing around won't assemble the parts. The parts must be assembled in a precise sequence, or the flagellum, eyeball, and pinky finger simply won't work. The assembly instructions are irreducibly complex.

But it gets still worse for evolution.

The design is irreducibly complex.

The assembly is irreducibly complex.

And even worse, the activation sequence is irreducibly complex too, because somebody has to pull the cord that gets the motor started, and somebody has to set the spring that powers the trap. And somebody has to put in the cheese.

New Scientist Magazine called the flagellum, "a prime example of a complex molecular system—an intricate nano machine beyond the craft of any human engineer" (Dan Jones, "Uncovering the Evolution of the Bacterial Flagellum," (Feb 16, 2008).

*The flagellum is a true nano-machine of remarkable complexity in structure and assembly control. This macromolecular machine self-assembles and repairs, displays assembly control and processing, operates with two gears, is fueled by proton motive force, and the apparatus is 'hard-wired' to a sensory apparatus that functions on short-term memory (chemotaxis). Rotor speeds for E. coli are estimated at 17,000 rpm but motors of some marine vibrios have been clocked upward of 100,000 rpm.*

— WILLIAM DEMBSKI, ED., DARWIN'S
NEMESIS, 2006, P. 215

If you were to pull out one of your hairs and cut it in half, 8 million of these nano machines would fit on the cross section.

Pause and consider.

Evolution and natural selection simply can't explain these complex machines, and how they evolved incrementally.

Atheistic evolutionists like Richard Dawkins are so messed up by all of this, that some of them, including Dawkins (who wrote *The God Delusion*) have started saying that life on earth was seeded by aliens. Who's crazy now? Who's atheistic desperation is showing?

When it comes to evolution, the motives are suspect. The complexity is beyond possibility. The irreducible complexity is a nail in the coffin. And there's one more problem I'd like to mention and then we're done.

---

*4. BEAUTY. Would you rather live in a world with, a) survival of the fittest, or b) the face of a loving Heavenly Father at its core?*

Ideas have consequences. Once you board the train of evolutionary theory, and the materialism that goes with it, you have to ride that train to its conclusion.

What is that conclusion?

Despair.

Because evolution makes the universe radically impersonal. It makes life meaningless. It makes humans into highly evolved animals. It makes all thought into chemical reactions based on chance.

There is no beauty, no love, no caring, no sin, no salvation, no Savior, no God, no heaven, no hell, and no justice in the end. Just random chance that came from God only knows where.

To board the train of evolution is to ride through a land of illusions on the tracks to despair.

I will set my life inside the story that tells of a God who loves me, and created me to enjoy his fellowship forever.

In the beginning, God created the heavens and the earth.

The Lord has appeared of old to me, saying: "Yes, I have loved you with an everlasting love; Therefore with lovingkindness I have drawn you." (Jeremiah 31:3)

That story is good enough for me.

# PLURALISM

Now while Paul waited for them at Athens, his
spirit was provoked within him when he saw that
the city was given over to idols. (Acts 17:16)

Paul was one of the most brilliant thinkers and
writers in the history of Christianity. He finds
himself in Athens, the major city of Greece, and his
spirit is "provoked within him."

This means he felt a giant ache in his heart for
the people of this great city. Along with that ache for
the city, he feels a righteous anger on behalf of God.

Why is Paul upset? Paul is upset because the city
is given over to idols. He finds innumerable statues
of countless deities. Idols lined the streets of Athens.
They sat on the shelves of every home. The Athenians worshiped hundreds and hundreds of gods.

Each one had power over their lives. These idols pulled the strings over their health, their wealth, their fertility, and their fate. Each one needed sacrifices, worship, prayers, regular feedings, and offerings.

The devil had spun such a web of lies around these people, they couldn't see their way out.

Many gods. Many views. Many philosophies. Many contradictory positions. All coexisting peacefully in the hearts of people too blind to see that none of this makes sense, and it can't be real. The people of Athens labor under a powerful, almost hypnotic, illusion.

They labored under the illusion called Pluralism.

## THE UNHOLY ANGLER

There is nothing new in the world. God doesn't change. Human nature doesn't change. Mankind's basic rebellion against God doesn't change.

The idea that many competing and even contradictory ideas can be true at the same time isn't something new. Paul faced it two thousand years ago in Athens and in every Gentile city he visited. Three thousand years ago the prophet Elijah faced it when the same people who worshiped the invisible God of the Jews also thought they could worship a competing idol named Baal.

This is not new. The same devil is spinning the same web of illusions he has been spinning since he questioned God back in the garden of Eden.

The devil is a fisherman. First, he lures you — that's the illusion. Then, he hooks you — that's the painful surprise. Then, he eats you (cf. 2 Peter 5:8) — he neutralizes you in the great spiritual warfare of the ages.

## WHAT IS PLURALISM?

This is tricky, because there is a *good pluralism*, which I want to affirm, and there's a *philosophical pluralism*, which I want to expose as an illusion.

Good pluralism simply means respectful disagreement. We don't agree on certain things. We don't like each other's views. Even so, we respect one another. We uphold each one's rights to express their views in appropriate ways. We allow for a pluralism of thought, opinion, belief, and practice. We celebrate our differences.

A good pluralist says, "I defend your right to be wrong." This is the opposite of shutting down the opposition. It flies in the face of the barrage of bullying-into-ideological-compliance we see today.

Bullying is the opposite of good pluralism. It's fascism, which is the rule of violence — a means of forcing people into your way of thinking.

As Christians, we stand for this good pluralism. If pluralism means diversity of opinion and thought coupled with mutual respect and toleration, then great! Scripture is all for that.

Even James Dobson, known for his highly conservative positions has said:

> It is very important to understand that pluralism is part of our system. We don't all think the same thing and part of our strength is that we come from different perspectives. We have to respect one another even when we disagree with each other. There has to be a spirit of tolerance for the views of others, while also being deeply committed to the positions we hold. If we do that, I think we can coexist and learn to love each other better.

So, good pluralism is not the pluralism I want to debunk. I want to talk about another concept.

*Philosophical pluralism.* That's the deadly illusion. Here's what that means:

> Pluralism is a sophisticated system of thought arguing that no religion or world view has the right to declare itself true, right, or superior to any other view, or to judge any other view as wrong (counterfactual), because mutually contradictory ideas can be equally valid and true.

Think of the word plural. It means more than one. Multiple.

Pluralism is the religion, the faith, or the conviction that there are multiple truths in *every* category.

Pluralism is the view that says it's wrong to say anything is wrong, because everything is right in some sense.

Ironically, there is one exception. There is one thing that is always wrong to say, which is to say that my system is right and therefore all others are wrong, because that would be a sin against the "plural." That is pluralism's unpardonable sin.

Good pluralism says, You're wrong, let's be friends.

Bad pluralism says, Nobody is ever wrong, except the one who labels my ideas as wrong.

It's called *Pluralism* because multiple, contradictory realities can be right, or right enough, even though they compete. Even though they contradict. Even though they are polar opposites of each other.


## WHAT ARE SOME FEATURES OF PLURALISM?

DOUBT: *Truth is a giant question mark.*

Pluralists aren't convinced anything is true. They're skeptical of everything. Skeptical of every authority.

Everything has question marks.

They glory in their "tolerance" for ambiguity.

They say you're rude, mean, unloving, or intolerant if you state your truth with any level of certainty.

For many generations, Christians and non-Christians basically have been in a tug of war over whose truth has more evidence. The Gospel versus the World. Which truth will win in the evidence game? Prove it.

Today, *nothing* is provable. Under pluralism, when Christians proclaim the gospel, we're immediately in trouble because we're so confident. Today's pluralists doubt that there is a truth to begin with. If there is truth, they're skeptical we can accurately find it. Correct and incorrect hardly matter at all.

Pluralism turns out to mean "faith in doubt."

---

*PROPAGANDA: Truth is something I bend to my desires. "There are no facts, only interpretations."*

Postmodernists feel we can never be truly objective because we carry a busload of biases, cultural prejudices, and the arrogance to believe that our way is the right way.

Over a century ago, philosopher Freidrich Nietzsche wrote, "There are no facts, only interpretations."

So, when we say that Jesus is the way to God, a pluralist receives that—and every other claim—as just one person's interpretation.

This is where we get the common statement: "That's true for you but not true for me."

*Everything* is propaganda — biased information to promote an agenda.

---

*SUBJECTIVE: Truth is something I feel inside.*

For most of our daily lives, we assume that "the truth is out there." It exists in the real world outside our minds. We don't prove this, we just assume it.

So an architect or engineer calculates roof trusses by referring to data outside his or her own "opinion." These are mathematical facts, and the roof can handle the snow load. Let's call this "objective truth."

"Subjective truth," in contrast, is the view that truth is shaped by personal tastes, opinions, and feelings.

Radical pluralists are less likely to ask, "Is it true?" and more likely to ask, "Does it feel right for you?"

Christians say that if you want to find what is true, open your Bible and look *outside* yourself to the revelation of the Word of God. Look outside yourself.

Pluralists say that if you want to find what is true, look *inside* yourself. Launch a voyage into inner space, and find your own truth. Because everybody has their own custom truth package.

It is certainly true that everybody has their own *perspective*. But, in the biblical worldview, perspective doesn't alter reality.

In case you think this is something new, I refer you to the book of Judges in the Old Testament, 3,500 years ago: "Everyone did what was right in his own eyes" (Judges 17:6). That is the soul of pluralism.

But what if selling a child into prostitution feels right in some cultures, or if dumping toxins into a river feels right for some corporate CEO's? A recent survey of girls in India showed that over half believed it was okay for a husband to beat his wife.

Well, that's not true for me, and I guarantee it's not true for you either.

This radical subjectivism has consequences. It makes truth...

RELATIVE: *Truth is local and limited, for my time, my place, and my people.*

In another time, it might not be true.

In another place, it might not be true.

In another culture, it might not be true.

Pluralism makes truth a moving target: it

depends on people, place, and time. There are very few permanent truths—called "absolutes"—for all people, all places, and all times. That's why our post-modern friends can say that Jesus might be true for you, but not for them. To them, it's all relative.

It is also...

---

CONTRADICTORY: *Truth can contradict itself.*

So a truth can be both true and false at the same time. And now, I have a splitting headache.

Have you seen the COEXIST bumper sticker? Each letter is the symbol of a different religion or worldview. On one hand, the COEXIST bumper sticker is a symbol of the good kind of pluralism — an open handed tolerance and patience we should all have with those with whom we disagree.

But philosophically, they simply can't all be true.

Think of the contradictions you have to accept to affirm "all religions say the same thing." The fact is that all religions say mutually contradictory things; that's why there are so many of them.

Christians teach a God who is a Trinity.

Muslims teach one God, and say that the Trinity is an insult against God.

The Athenians in Paul's day taught a multitude of separate gods.

And Hindus say all is god and god is all.

They can't all be right. The whole realm of logic would evaporate into a misty haze if they were all right.

Except under pluralism. It's like taking ten thousand puzzles, taking one random piece from each box, and trying to fit them all together. The only way to do it is to cram together pieces that don't fit. And if you do, the picture will make no sense. It is absurd. It is incoherent.

There's a better bumper sticker. It uses the same images to spell out the word *CONTRADICT*. Because they can't all be right.

## BACK TO ATHENS

Athens, in Paul's day, was a city full of idols and a culture full of thinkers. The philosophies that built western civilization came from that place and that time.

Yet somehow, they are able to hold together that which cannot be held together. What does Paul say?

> Therefore he reasoned in the synagogue with the Jews and with the Gentile worshipers, and in the marketplace daily with those who happened to be there. (Acts 17:17)

He reasoned with them. He didn't isolate from them. He didn't run from them. He didn't stand on the corner with signs and yell at them. He went to their marketplace, and reasoned with them. And he did this daily. He didn't just unload everything at once. He dripped his content out. He made the case. He spoke to those who were willing to listen.

St. Paul patiently, gently, and wisely made the case that there is a God in heaven, a Savior who came to earth, and a salvation gift that lasts forever. He delivered these truths into a culture that suffered the snake bite of pluralism, and was descending into death at breakneck speed.

## WHAT CAN CHRISTIANS SAY TO OUR PLURALISTIC FRIENDS?

*SCRIPTURE: First, to the Pluralists in the Church, we say Listen to the Testimony of Christ and the Scripture.*

If you take the Bible at face value, you'll never come up with anything like universalism.

> Jesus said to him, "I am the way, the truth, and the life. No one comes to the Father except through Me." (John 14:6)

Paul was respectful of the Athenians as people, though he called their religious views "ignorant" (Acts 17:16-34).

God's prophet, Elijah, mocked the priests of the regional god, Baal and called people to choose between the True God and false gods (1 Kings 18:21-40).

King David called gods of the other nations "demons" (Psalm 106:35-37).

St. Paul echoed David when he claimed that everybody who worships an idol is really worshipping a "demon" (an evil spirit, 1 Corinthians 10:21).

Though God's people respected their neighbors, they flat-out rejected their neighbor's religions. No matter how long you scan the Bible's horizons, you'll never find a glimmer of pluralism. The church must steer clear of all religious, biblical, and philosophical pluralism, even as we defend our neighbor's right to disagree with us.

The pluralists in the world need to wrestle with a few things too.

---

*IMPRACTICAL: Pluralism simply doesn't work in the real world.*

Pluralism stands against everything we know from science, logic, and experience. It stands against the Bible.

> Jesus said: "But everyone who hears these sayings of Mine, and does not do them, will be like a foolish man who built his house on the sand..." (Matthew 7:26)

There's a story of an atheist-pluralist-scientist-man who became an expert in harvesting mushrooms. If you eat the wrong mushroom, you die. So he trained under the best mushroom experts (mycologists) he could find, and became an expert himself.

One day, he realized that pluralism and mycology could never go together.

*"Faith in Doubt"* wouldn't work, because if there were any doubt in a mushroom being edible, that doubt could be deadly.

Labelling everything his teachers told him *"propaganda"* would also be deadly. The idea that everything is opinion, and there are no facts, just interpretations, is simply not going to work. In the realm of picking mushrooms, there are unarguable facts, with no room for interpretation.

A *subjective* approach to truth wouldn't work either. He couldn't unearth a truffle and look inside himself to see "how he felt" about it. He had to know for sure, based on external evidence, if it was edible, or deadly.

Same thing for truth being *relative*. If this mushroom is deadly, it is deadly for this time and every time, for this place and every place, and for this culture and every culture, for this person and every person.

Even more, the whole idea of truth being *self-contradictory* was out the window too. A mushroom can't be both edible and not edible at the same time. It's one or the other, not both.

This atheist became a Christian. Because God can use fungi to glorify the name of Jesus.

It might be a fun debate in a university classroom, but Pluralism is a philosophy that never works in the real world.

Every time you walk into a building, an engineer has calculated the roof trusses. What if those engineers used pluralistic thinking? You would never want to be in that building during a blizzard.

Back in Chicago, I taught a Bible study on a cold, rainy Wednesday night. Afterwards, a man came up to me, dripping wet. He said, "I left my lights on and my battery is dead. Can you give me a jump?"

"Sure," I said. I have cables.

So we went outside into a cold, driving rain. The only light came from a parking lot light nearby.

I gave him the cables, told him to hook them up to his battery, and I ran over to my car, drove it over, and popped the hood.

I got out, he handed me my end of the jumper cables.

Before I hooked them up, I double checked. I said, "Red to positive, right?" "Definitely," he said. "Red to positive."

Now, let's pause here. Is there any way that a pluralistic philosophy works in this situation? You can have all the armchair philosophical debates you want. You can come up with all the logic in the world why truths can contradict and reality is plural.

At the end of the day, it's binary. True or false. Right or wrong. Red to positive or red to negative.

The instant I touched the cable to my battery, it snapped and sparked and made me jump back. After I got my heart rate under control, I checked. Red to negative. Oops. His *opinion* didn't make a difference. His opinion was sinking sand. His sincerity didn't make a difference either. This is the problem with pluralism.

In actual practice, the only way a pluralist can live in the real world is by borrowing the Christian worldview in order to survive. Reality is the rock that God describes. Reality is the bedrock of Jesus and his Word.

---

*HEARTBREAKING: The human spirit cannot thrive in a world where truth won't stay true.*

Pluralists are stuck claiming one thing in theory and living another thing in practice. This breaks their heart.

Listen to these famous atheists at the end of their days:

- Jean Paul Sartre: "I reached out for religion, I longed for it, it was the remedy... I needed a Creator." [*The Words*, 102]

- Albert Camus: "For anyone who is alone, without God and without a master, the weight of days is dreadful." [*The Fall*, 133.]
- Nietzsche: "Speak. What wilt thou, unknown-god?... Do come back with all the tortures. To the last of all that are lonely, O, come back! Oh, come back, my unknown God! My pain! My last happiness!" [*Thus Spoke Zarathustra*, pt 4]
- David Hume: "I dine, I play a game of backgammon, I converse...; and when after three or four hours' amusement, I would return to these speculations, they appear so cold, so strained, and ridiculous, that I cannot find in my heart to enter into them any farther." [*A Treatise on Human Nature*, 1.4.7.]
- Will Durant: "I survive morally because I retain the moral code that was taught me along with the religion, while I discarded the religion.... You and I are living on a shadow.... But what will happen to our children...? They are living on the shadow of a shadow. [*Chicago Sun-Times* 8/24/75 1B]

It is said that Sartre regretted how many young

people he turned to atheism. Before his death, he began visiting a Christian pastor. He wrote, "I do not feel that I am the product of chance, a speck of dust in the universe, but someone who was expected, prepared, prefigured. In short, a being whom only a Creator could put here." (*National Review*, 11 June, 1982, p. 677).

God designed you for truth.

Jesus said, "I am the truth" (John 14:6).

His person is truth incarnated.

His life is truth authenticated.

His teaching is truth communicated.

His gospel is truth activated.

His Church is truth propagated.

His Kingdom is truth emancipated.

Jesus is the truth. And he alone can satisfy the quest of every human heart.

---

*FRAGMENTED: Life can't make sense without a unifying core, and that unifying core is the Lord Jesus Christ.*

Pluralism robs the world of a unifying core. It takes the things that are precious — the things that give life meaning — and makes them all plural, as if reality is an eat-what-you-want buffet.

What are these things that make life precious? God. Value. Truth. Life. Purpose. Love. The Gospel.

But pluralism makes them plural. It proposes an ever changing menu of...

Gods without A God.

Values without Value.

Truths without Truth.

Lives without Life.

Purposes without Purpose. (What is the purpose of your purposes?)

Loves without Love.

Gospels without a Gospel of a Savior who lived and died and lived again to reconcile a sinful race to God.

Jesus came as a Teacher and a Prophet. He came to deliver *words*. Those who would be loyal to him must be willing to affirm that God has revealed himself in both Jesus Christ as a person, and equally in the content and words of his teachings — the Bible. To distort the shape of God's reality isn't just a mistake, it's rebellious and sinful.

Pluralism attempts to negate the Bible. It is the source of the great sadness, confusion, and despair in our world today.

There is one body and one Spirit, just as you were called in one hope of your calling; one Lord, one faith, one baptism; one God and Father of all, who is above all, and through all, and in you all. (Ephesians 4:4-6)

Think of it this way. The devil is the world's first pluralist. He whispered to Eve that God's way wasn't the only way. Humans have been suffering ever since Adam and Eve took that bait.

But truth is singular, not plural. Following that singular, bedrock truth is the only way back home.

# PERFECTIONISM

We live in a twisted world, wildly distorted in everything that matters most. Our culture has a twisted view of truth, of human nature, of right and wrong, and of God. All of these distortions mess with our lives. They add up to a painfully distorted view of ourselves.

When you look in the mirror are you seeing what the world sees or what God sees?

One of the most alluring, yet painful, lies of the world-system is the lie that tells us that unless we're perfect we won't be loved.

Perfect complexion. Perfect body. Perfect spouse, children, house, and car. The pressures have never been greater, especially on students. Today's adolescent culture-of-cruelty finds the tiniest flaw in a person, and tears at it like a vulture on road kill. It is enormously difficult to get through high school without emotional scars, most of them scabbing over the imperfections, real or perceived, in our lives. Perfection is a horrible taskmaster.

Let's see what God's Word says about the illusion of perfectionism.

## WHAT IS PERFECTIONISM?

*Perfectionism is the excessive fear of rejection for not being perfect.*

Fear is excessive whenever your fear freezes your growth and hurts your relationships. It's the kind of fear that oozes out through all your pores, and paralyzes you into indecision and keeping a low profile. I have painful memories going back to childhood.

I played Little League Baseball. I was a great fielder, and a lousy batter. I could run down any fly ball in center field. But I couldn't hit the ball.

Actually, that's not exactly right.

I didn't hit the ball, because I didn't swing the bat.

Picture adorable little Billy, maybe 8 or 9 years old, up at bat. I just stood there and hoped for a walk. I refused to swing my bat.

The nice thing was that it was little league, so half the time I got a walk, which was a pretty decent fifty percent on base percentage.

All my teammates stood there cheering for me. *Come on Bill, just try. Just swing the bat!*

After a couple of at bats, the other teams knew they could stand around and wait. They put on the "Pansy Shift," which means the fielders all came in close enough for me to spit on. I remember one time, when a third baseman sat down on his glove and rested while I batted.

That was special.

When the game was over, I would go home to my Dad, who had played pro-baseball in the minor leagues for the Chicago Cubs, and he would ask how I did. I would say one walk and one strikeout or whatever.

I was always glad that my dad hardly ever came to games. Not because I didn't love him, but because I was afraid of letting him down.

One author reached out on social media, to ask for examples of perfectionism. The response was overwhelming. How about a small sample:

- Doing all the household chores because that way they will be done right. Then feeling resentful because no one ever offers to help and here she is, doing all the work herself. [C.S. Lewis named this person "Mrs. Fidget" — Google it.]
- Rearranging the dishes in the dishwasher to her standards.
- After my mother vacuumed the living room floor, if she found footprints in the

carpet, she lined us up and measured our feet to the prints. The culprit was made to bear the shame of messing up her hard work and had to re-vacuum the floor.

- Correcting details in your wife's stories.
- Never letting your kid hammer a nail because they won't make it go in right.
- People with perfectionism have a look of disapproval frozen on their face.
- People who drive in the fastest lane and go exactly the speed limit, trying to control others' behavior [Author's Note: There's a hot spot in hell for those people.]
- Staying up all night to clean for a party because someone might see one speck of dirt, or one thing out of place (as if someone is going to look in every corner of your house).

There were a bunch of religious perfectionists in Jesus' day. They were hyper-religious people called Pharisees. One day, they tested Jesus.

Jesus returned to the Mount of Olives, but early the next morning he was back again at the Temple. A crowd soon gathered, and he sat down and taught them. As he was speaking, the teachers of religious law and Pharisees brought a woman they had caught in the act of adultery. They put her in front of the crowd. "Teacher," they said to Jesus, "this woman was caught in the very act of adultery. The law of Moses says to stone her. What do you say?" They were trying to trap him into saying something they could use against him, but Jesus stooped down and wrote in the dust with his finger. (John 8:1-6, NLT)

So here is a test. This woman has failed. She has failed the test of moral perfection, and the penalty—in that nation, under their law, at that time—is death.

We'll get back to her story.

## WHAT ARE SOME FEATURES OF PERFECTIONISM?

*VARIETIES: Different kinds of fear make different kinds of perfectionism.*

It's a variety pack.

*Fear of Rejection.* This fear never goes away. But it's really hard in your teens and twenties.

Your looks, your complexion, your hair, your body shape, your grades, your popularity, how athletic.

It's a crazy painful game, and everybody's playing it.

- *Fear of Failure.* That was me and baseball.

- *Fear of Losing Face.* That is still me and dancing. And public singing. And preaching. and just about everything else.
- *Fear of Losing Control.* Produces control freaks.
- *Fear of Not Fitting In.*
- *Fear of Loss, of Poverty, of Relapsing to your old ways.*
- *Fear of germs.* (Monk, Felix Unger)
- *Fear of Exposure, Fear of Public Humiliation.* That's what the woman felt when he dragged her to Jesus and threw her on the ground. Public humiliation.

These are the fears that make people overcompensate. They make people work themselves to death trying to achieve the impossible. These fears wear a thousand masks.

These fears are real. They are powerful. They make sense. You are not ungodly or evil if you live with these fears.

God isn't mad at you.

Whatever look of disapproval you may sense on the face of the perfectionists in your life, that is not the look on God's face when he thinks of you. God loves you, and if you have Jesus, God approves of you just as much as he approves of Jesus Christ.

*QUEST: Humans have been longing for perfection ever since the Garden of Eden.*

When God created humans, he created us with our own kind of perfection. Perfect health. Perfect bodies. Perfect hair. Perfect complexion. Perfect minds. Perfect morality. Perfect love.

No fears. No masks. No straining and sweating to try to fit in. No controlling behaviors.

Just pure joy and innocence and love in the perfection of God's original creation.

> And they were both naked, the man and his wife,
> and were not ashamed. (Genesis 2:25)

We have no way of knowing how many years or even centuries that perfection lasted in the Garden of Eden. But we do know Adam and Eve had one terrible, horrible, no good, very bad day.

Adam and Eve threw a giant rock though the window of perfection, and all of their original perfection shattered into a million pieces.

That rock is called sin.

Sin is the root. All the fears and mess with your tiny little brain grow out of that original sin on that horrible day. The whole human race was messed up. Everybody.

Yes, all the perfect people in your life too. No one and nothing was spared the brokenness of original sin, and no one and nothing maintains its original perfection except God.

We live in Paradise Lost.

The moment in history when Adam sinned is called the Fall.

In the Fall, we humans lost our perfection and have been longing for it ever since.

That's a problem because...

---

*IMPOSSIBLE: Perfectionists spin their wheels in the pursuit of the impossible.*

Paradise Lost doesn't become Paradise Regained until Jesus returns. When he returns, he will reverse the curse of sin. He will yank it out of our beings by the root. And he will restore all the original awesomeness that was lost in the fall.

Until then, pimples happen. You miss the winning shot. You get rejected by the person of your dreams. The puppy poops on your favorite rug.

> I have told you all this so that you may have peace in me. Here on earth you will have many trials and sorrows. But take heart, because I have overcome the world." (John 16:33, NLT)

What did Jesus say you will have in this world? "Many trials and sorrows."

Sorry.

It's a tough world. It's a morally broken Pain Machine.

What makes it tougher is the illusion that you can make the tough stuff go away.

You're going to strike out. You're going to be embarrassed. You're going to mess up. You're going to fail the comparison test. You're going to feel ignored on social media. You're going to lose money. You're going to have relationship problems. You're going to deal with all the pains of a fallen, broken, messed up world. You're going to get yelled at. You're going to get interrupted by weirdoes. You're going to lose face. You're going to smell bad. You're going to get a germ on your food. You're going to have a messy house. You're going to fail a test. You're going to play the wrong note. You're going to get flabby or bony or tired or weak. You're going to feel pain. You're going to get sick. You're going to get caught in a sin, just like the lady who was dragged before Jesus.

You can't control it all away. You can't scrub it all away. You can't slap on a smiley face and pretend it away.

You can't even pray it away.

No, you can't.

Say it with me:

*I live as an imperfect person surrounded by imperfect people in a radically imperfect world.*

*And God loves me anyway.*

---

*RESULT: The main result of perfectionism is putting Judgment and Condemnation at the Core of your emotions and your relationships.*

Perfectionism is negativity in overdrive. It spews forth toxins in three directions:

*1. I condemn myself.* What do you say to yourself about yourself when you fail? *I'm stupid. I'm ugly. I don't matter. I'm worthless. I'm not good enough. If I fail nobody will be my friend.* This is the hiss of perfectionism.

*2. Other people condemn me.* These are the labels other people put on you. Some are real, some are imagined. *Everybody hates me. Nobody wants me. They think I'm horrible, ugly, or stupid.*

*3. I condemn you.* This is how a perfectionist makes life bearable. If you focus enough on other people's failures, maybe your failures won't feel so bad. This is the genesis of a critical spirit.

All of this drives people away from the perfectionist. In a sad way, this just might be the goal, because the devil has you convinced you can be safe that way. In some cases, perfectionism is an imperfect person's unconscious strategy to keep the world at arm's length.

To love is to risk. To live is to risk. And it is better to try than to out of fear of failure not try at all.

Perfectionism is a nasty tyrant that won't let you be okay with not being okay. Perfectionism will never let you rest. It notes every imperfection and rubs it raw.

Perfectionism is the little engine in your soul that is opposite of grace. It wears you out.

## WHAT DOES GOD SAY TO MY INNER PERFECTIONIST?

There stands Jesus. Perfectionists crowd around him. A woman grovels at his feet. She is imperfect in ways that every single person understands. There is nowhere to run. Nowhere to hide. She is humiliated. She is afraid.

What does Jesus say to that crowd, and what does Jesus say to that painfully imperfect person?

To the crowd, he says this:

They kept demanding an answer, so he stood up again and said, "All right, stone her. But let those who have never sinned throw the first stones!" Then he stooped down again and wrote in the dust. When the accusers heard this, they slipped away one by one, beginning with the oldest, until only Jesus was left in the middle of the crowd with the woman. (John 8:7-9, NLT)

All the perfectionists dropped their stones and went away.

Why? Because Jesus simply reminded them of their own imperfections.

All those critical voices in your head are in *everybody's* head at one time or another. You're not weird, and you're not horrible, and you're not worthless, and you're not evil, and you're not unforgivable, and you're not beyond redemption.

There is nobody without sin.

There is none who measures up. Not even one. This is reality, and the sooner you embrace it, the easier your life will be.

Here's what Jesus would say to your Inner Perfectionist.

---

*GRACE: Because of Calvary Love, any part of your heart that makes you condemn and control and criticize yourself and others is not the spirit of Christ.*

The spirit of Christ is the spirit of Grace.

So now, it's just Jesus and this imperfect woman. Look at what he says to her:

> When Jesus had raised Himself up and saw no one but the woman, He said to her, "Woman, where are those accusers of yours? Has no one condemned you?" She said, "No one, Lord." And

Jesus said to her, "Neither do I condemn you; go and sin no more." (John 8:10, 11)

The spirit of Christ is the spirit of Grace.

Jesus calls her, "Woman." This is a term of dignity and respect. Everybody else treated her as an object—a tool for their theological shenanigans. Jesus treated her, even in her most shameful moment, as a sacred person, created in the image of God.

When I say Calvary, I mean the hill where Jesus died on the Cross. When I say Calvary Love, I mean everything that Jesus did on that Cross. Because Jesus dying on the Cross is the ONLY REASON, God could speak this grace into that woman's heart.

It all goes back to the Cross. It always does.

*The heart of Scripture is Christ. The heart of Christ is grace. The heart of Grace is the Cross.*

It doesn't matter where the condemnation-daggers are coming from. From yourself. From your parents, teachers, boss, or peers. Jesus Christ came to tell you once for all, there is therefore now NO CONDEMNATION for those who are in Christ Jesus (Romans 8:1). Those voices don't come from God. You don't have to listen to them for even one more day.

And don't miss the order of Christ's statements to this precious woman. First, he frees her from condemnation. Only then does he instruct her to go and sin no more. This order is immeasurably important. Until the voices of condemnation are silenced, the power of sin can never be broken. God never tells a person, stooped under the weight of condemnation, to go and sin no more. First, he rolls away the guilt and shame, and only then does he invite them to a transformed life.

Jesus pronounced her forgiven before she improved her life even one little bit.

Grace first.

Life-change after.

---

FORGIVENESS: *Because of Calvary Love, you are already forgiven all your imperfections and failures.*

They have been washed away from God's sight forever.

I don't know what guilt or shame you carry within you. I don't know your secrets. I don't know the stuff you've done you wish you could undo.

But I know there is forgiveness with God, and that is the only reason I can keep walking with him day by day.

I heard an old preacher say that if you knew what was in my heart, and how nasty and dark I can be, you wouldn't waste your time listening to me.

But that's okay. Because if I knew all the nastiness that was in your heart, I wouldn't waste my time writing or preaching to you!

When Jesus died, he paid the penalty for all that stuff. He suffered. He died. He washed you white as snow.

> "Come now, and let us reason together," Says the LORD, "Though your sins are like scarlet, They shall be as white as snow; Though they are red like crimson, They shall be as wool. (Isaiah 1:18)

Jesus wants to speak forgiveness to your inner perfectionist, inner critic, inner judge and jury. He wants to tell you the pressure is off, once for all, forever, because of Calvary Love.

---

*AWESOMENESS: Because of Calvary Love, God sees the awesomeness, coolness, capability, and beauty of the person he's making you to be.*

Here is the world's coolest, weirdest Bible verse:

> You shall no longer be termed Forsaken, Nor shall your land any more be termed Desolate; But you shall be called Hephzibah, and your land Beulah; For the LORD delights in you, And your land shall be married. (Isaiah 62:4)

Let's decode this, especially the Hebrew words, *Hephzibah* and Beulah. *Here's* what it all means:

Just when you feel totally rejected, just when you feel totally unloved, God swoops in, and sweeps you off your feet and he says you're beautiful to him.

He calls you *Hephzibah*, which means you make God happy whenever he looks at you.

He calls you *Beulah*, which means you are beautiful to him, like a bride or groom dressed for your wedding day.

He says you are Not Forsaken; you are connected to God. He delights in you.

How did he come to see you this way?

Christ washed you. Christ performed a spiritual makeover on you, and whatever ugliness marred your beauty has been swept away. He robed you in glorious robes of beauty. He decked you in absolute perfection.

He did this for you; you can't do it for yourself. Let go.

When Christ was crucified, he absorbed whatever ugliness clung to you. He buried it forever in a sea of forgetfulness. He also flung a royal robe over you, woven with his own goodness, righteousness, and beauty. To God, you look just like Jesus. So now you are perfect in God's eyes. No matter what you do or don't do or start doing or stop doing.

It's grace. Be secure.

Your sins won't stick to you. Your tears won't

make you ugly to God. The marks on your body, the weakness in your bones, the failure of your systems, the brokenness mapped in your eyes, and the sadness of your smile... none of these change the fact of your awesomeness in the eyes of God. His heart melts over you. He rejoices over you with "leaps of joy" (Zephaniah 3:17).

All your perfection is in him. Just believe.

---

*GROWTH: Because of Calvary Love, I can grow in self-esteem and self-confidence even in the face of failure, rejection, and tough times.*

Success is not the attainment of perfection but the continuance of growth.

Self-esteem doesn't come from being praised all the time, like a perfect little snowflake.

Self-esteem doesn't come from trophies.

Self-esteem comes from a) growing deeper and deeper in how God sees you, and b) living from that place, especially after you fail. Get up and try again. Get up, don't pout, don't whine, don't quit. Overcome adversity, don't run from it. You can do it. You can accomplish great things with your life.

> What then shall we say to these things? If God is
> for us, who can be against us? (Romans 8:31)

So Blunder Forward! Relax your grip. Unclench your spirit. Get dirt on your clothes and spill your drink on the kitchen table. The world will keep spinning and God will keep on loving you.

So will the decent people in your life.

Your imperfections don't define you — that's an illusion from the dysfunction of your past. It's God's grace that defines you. His opinion is the deepest, truest reality in your life. Grow in your faith and knowledge of your identity and privileges as his child. That's the secret an invincible spirit.

It all starts by knowing Christ, resting in Calvary love, and then blundering forward because even if you fail, you just can't lose.

# UTOPIANISM

The Emerald City. Shangri-La. Atlantis. Camelot. Wakanda. The Shire. Asgard. Avalon. The human heart longs for perfect society and has created plenty of mythological ones. Ever since Adam and Eve exited the Garden of Eden, our hearts have longed to return.

But Paradise was lost — not simply the physical place, but even more importantly, the Paradise of intimate fellowship with God.

Can we return? Some say yes, and apply their efforts to create Utopia. The Bible, however, presents a pessimistic picture of worldly society as long as it remains without the personal presence of Jesus.

> For we know that the whole creation groans and labors with birth pangs together until now. (Romans 8:22)

This is a blanket statement about "the whole creation." It applies to the whole cosmos and everything in it. From the most distant galaxies of the universe, to the tiniest sub-atomic particle on the bottom of the sea. Everything big. Everything small. Every rock, tree, plant, and field. Every animal and every human.

It applies to your school. Your cafeteria, locker room, and math class. It applies to your job and to traffic. The Whole Creation.

The whole creation groans and labors with birth pains. There is agony and struggle and suffering — but it's *birth* pains, so there is also hope of something beautiful yet to come after all the pain.

The great question of the ages is about exactly *who* can bring about the beautiful outcome of creation's labor. A colossal tug of war has been waged in answer to this question. Some say humans can bring about a good and just society. Some say it's humans by God's power. Some say it's God's power alone, without human power. To top it off, the Devil says he can do it.

So who's right?

Who will bring about humankind's dream of heaven on earth? What about Utopia?

## WHAT IS UTOPIANISM?

*Utopianism is the confidence that humans, working together, can usher in a period of perfect peace and prosperity and can make the world a better place.*

The word Utopia was coined by an author in the 1500s. In A.D. 1516, an English lawyer and philosopher named Sir Thomas More wrote a book called *Utopia*. In it, he described a fictional island society off the coast of South America where everything was always beautiful and peaceful and good.

The opposite of Utopia is dystopia. There are a lot of movies with dystopian futures: *The Hunger Games, Mad Max, The Matrix*, the *Divergent* movies, *Mazerunner*... Even *Wall-E*. In a dystopian future, societies completely break down and turn nasty.

Utopian societies evolve into awesomeness. Basically, Utopianism is a wildly optimistic view of the future based on human progress and human ideals.

## WHAT ARE SOME FEATURES OF UTOPIANISM?

*PHILOSOPHY: Utopian philosophy suggest that humans can create a beautiful world without reference to God.*

Almost always, utopianism is humanistic, and therefore atheistic.

When you apply the theory of evolution to *biology*, you get Darwinianism, or the evolution of species. Species improve as time goes on.

When you apply the theory of evolution to *society*, you get Utopianism. Society improves as time goes on. Medicine improves, so we get healthier. Our intelligence improves, so we get nicer to each other. We're evolving upward and better all the time.

I guess they haven't noticed the news lately.

Utopianism, or some version of it, is the goal of world government. This is the view that is being taught to most children in most public school systems. This is the assumption — an unproven, philosophy — that lies at the heart of how most people view society and government.

But there's a glitch in this assumption.

The idea that humans can create a better society without reference to God has never worked in the real world. In fact, in any society and in any culture, when the God of the Bible is followed, society improves. When atheism is followed, *tyranny* rises.

That is why the founders of the United States grounded their political theory by saying humans are endowed by their Creator with unalienable rights. Because God gave us our rights, no government can take them away—overturning millennia of historical precedent. That was the idea.

Most utopian ideas are humanism-based. There is nothing higher than a fully functional human being, they say. They have yet to answer the question how fallen, corrupt humans can create an un-fallen, un-corrupt utopia in which all of life is honored.

*BELIEF SYSTEM: Utopian philosophies offer competing visions of how the ideal society actually will happen, based on their belief systems.*

There are a whole lot of theories as to how this beautiful world will come about. Here is a short list of utopian theories: "there are socialist, capitalist, monarchical, democratic, anarchist, ecological, feminist, patriarchal, egalitarian, hierarchical, racist, left-wing, right-wing, reformist, free love, nuclear family, extended family, gay, lesbian, and many more utopias" (Lyman Tower Sargent).

I would add "technological utopianism" which says that technology, surrounding our lives, and even soon implanted in our brains, can bring about a perfect society.

People will be lining up for the Mark of the Beast. Imagine the excited conversation.

"Oh, it's so convenient and safe and fast! Gotta get me one of those!"

"And no more identity theft too!"

*OPTIMISTIC: Utopian philosophy sees a better, brighter, more beautiful society and has a positive outlook on the future.*

The world can be daisies and sunshine if we

work together. If only we can lay down our petty differences, we can make the world a better place. This is the thought process behind utopianism.

The only problem is that we all have different ideas of what makes the world a better place. What the utopian idealist calls "petty differences" the freedom-loving pragmatist calls "individuality and cherished personal preference."

Because we all have different ideas of the ideal life, utopianism requires that somebody choose whose idea of a better world wins in the end. For most of history, that choice, unfortunately, has been made by force: *This is our idea of a better world, and now we're going to cram it down your throats.*

Usually, this happens in the name of the greater good, but in actuality it only benefits those at the top.

---

*CHRISTIAN UTOPIANISM: There is a Christian version of Utopianism that includes God. It is called Post-Millennialism.*

The Bible teaches there is a coming period of wonderful peace and awesome prosperity. It is called the Millennium.

Now it will come about that In the last days The mountain of the house of the Lord Will be established as the chief of the mountains, And will be raised above the hills; And all the nations will stream to it. And many peoples will come and say, "Come, let us go up to the mountain of the Lord, To the house of the God of Jacob; That He may teach us concerning His ways And that we may walk in His paths." For the law will go forth from Zion And the word of the Lord from Jerusalem. And He will judge between the nations, And will render decisions for many peoples; And they will hammer their swords into plowshares and their spears into pruning hooks Nation will not lift up sword against nation, And never again will they learn war. (Isaiah 2:2-4)

The wolf also shall dwell with the lamb, The leopard shall lie down with the young goat, The calf and the young lion and the fatling together; And a little child shall lead them. (Isaiah 11:6)

Things that eat each other will turn vegan.

Scripture describes a thousand-year reign of Christ, called the Millennium. The Bible promised it, and that day is coming. I believe, along with most evangelical Christians, that the only way the millennium can happen is by Jesus coming again.

When Jesus comes, he will ride down with the armies of heaven. He will come visibly, bodily, and personally to planet earth. He will destroy the enemies of God and suck the evil out of our planet. Jesus Christ will personally rule and reign on earth for a thousand years. In this time, there will be Utopia. Ideal society. Perfect peace. Total prosperity. No crime. No war. No hunger. No poverty. No injustice.

That is what the Bible teaches.

Jesus comes back *before* the millennium can happen, so this view is called pre-millennialism. There is some disagreement, but this is the faith of millions of Christians.

*Pre-millennialism: Jesus comes back and ushers in the millennium (ideal society on earth).*

Post-millennialism is different. Post-millennialism teaches that by the power of God, we Christians can create Utopia *before* Jesus returns. Post-millennialists say the power of the gospel will transform the world. It can create an ideal society. We — God's people — will usher in the kingdom of God. We will usher in the millennium. We will bring heaven to earth. The Church, by God's power, will inaugurate a Golden Age of Prosperity and Peace. Only then, *after* we complete that mission, can Jesus return.

*Post-millennialism: the Church and the Gospel usher in the millennium, and then Jesus returns.*

Here is my position: If you're a lawyer, and you want to argue a case from the Bible itself, the only way to win the argument is to argue for pre-millennialism. I want to show you why. I also want to explain how we answer this idea that humans can usher in Utopia.

## WHAT CAN WE SAY TO OUR UTOPIAN FRIENDS?

To answer this question, I would like to go through a paragraph of Scripture with you, verse by verse, and comment as we go.

> For I consider that the sufferings of this present time are not worthy to be compared with the glory which shall be revealed in us. For the earnest expectation of the creation eagerly waits for the revealing of the sons of God. (Romans 8:18)

Notice the phrase, "this present time." There was a past time, there is this present time, and there is a future time. The central feature of this present time is the very depressing word, "sufferings." The first thing we would say to our utopian friends is this:

1. *This fallen world is a morally broken pain machine.*

No amount of effort will change this. No government. No politics. No church program. No evangelism program. Even if everybody on earth received Jesus as their Savior, it still wouldn't flip the switch of the machine of the giant pain machine into the off position.

The world was not created this way. God created it with beauty and order. Planet earth was created a Paradise. Utopia. The Garden of Eden, the Garden of God.

One day, God will fix it. He will turn it all around.

In fact, all creation stands on tiptoe waiting for that day. Right now, there is a twist in the fabric of the universe. There is a twist in the moral makeup of our being. But one day, God will straighten things out.

That day features the "revealing" of the sons and daughters of God.

That's our glorious destiny. It is future tense. But right now, we are caught inside a present-tense pain machine. And the next verse explains how that happened.

When Adam and Eve sinned, the whole creation fell under a curse.

For the creation was subjected to futility, not willingly, but because of Him who subjected it in hope; because the creation itself also will be delivered from the bondage of corruption into the glorious liberty of the children of God. For we know that the whole creation groans and labors with birth pains together until now. (Romans 8:20-22)

Scripture affirms, "creation was subjected to futility." Futility means "unattainment."

Think about that for a moment. Unattainment. Unobtainment. You can't get what you want. You can't get total fulfillment. You can't get total peace. You can't attain all your dreams. This world isn't Disneyworld and dreams don't aways come true.

Because creation was subject to unattainment, which means utopianism can never come true. God's Word is clear on this.

Verse 21 says we are trapped in "the bondage of corruption." Bondage, means we're stuck in it. And corruption means death, decay, disease, despair, destruction.

Let's not pity ourselves as if we were innocent victims of Adam and Eve, because we are not. This curse of unattainment, and this bondage to corruption is the inevitable consequence of a revolution against God. We all own at least a piece of that.

It is satanic in origin, human in expression, and arrogant by definition.

Look at the phrases God uses to describe the world in which we live:

- subjected to futility
- the bondage of corruption
- groans and labors

This fallen world is a morally broken world, and we can't fix it.

---

*2. Human Sin makes Utopia impossible.*

There is no other way to interpret Romans 8 and the rest of the Bible.

Does that mean we give up trying to heal the world's pain?

No way! The history of the world will show that no single group has done more to alleviate the world's pain than Christians. We're the ones who invented orphanages and hospitals. We fought to abolish slavery in the western world. We fought against child labor. We have given training and jobs and hopes to those trapped in prostitution. We built hospitals in the world's darkest, most dangerous places. Christians have been on the front lines of literacy, healthcare, and helping the impoverished, for two thousand years.

But not because we believe we can change the world.

It is because we believe God can change lives by the power of the gospel of the Lord Jesus Christ.

Yes, we pray and serve and work for transformation of institutions. We work to make government righteous. We get into schools and art and education and business and we bring the light of Jesus there.

But we never forget that the world's transformation won't be complete until the Lord returns, because the human heart remains corrupted by sin, so all our institutions are corrupted too.

Which leads to the third thing we would say to our Utopian friends, is:

---

*3. Apart from the return of Christ, there is no hope for fixing the deep wounds of our world.*

It is not just a problem of how we think, or of what we believe, or of how much money we throw at it, or of distribution, or of equalization, or of a lack of prayer, or of lack of love.

It is a problem with our very essence, and until that essence is *transformed*, utopia remains tantalizingly out of reach.

> Not only that, but we also who have the firstfruits of the Spirit, even we ourselves groan within ourselves, eagerly waiting for the adoption, the redemption of our body. (Romans 8:23)

There's the transformation we long for. We

suffer, we acutely feel the painful gap between what is ideal and what is real. So we eagerly look forward to a future day called the "adoption," a.k.a. "the redemption of our body."

What does that mean?

That is the day when Jesus returns and yanks all the residue of sin out of us by the roots, once for all, body, soul, and spirit.

- *When you received Jesus, God saved you from the PENALTY of Sin.*
- *As you grow in the Lord, God delivers you from the POWER of Sin.*
- *When he returns, he will deliver you from the PRESENCE of Sin.*

That will be Utopia. That is when paradise is regained. That is when the lion lies with the lamb. That is when the Lord Jesus himself will fix the deep wounds of this world. With one almighty word proceeding from his mouth, all the things we hoped for, all the things we fought for and labored for, and prayed for — with one word out of the mouth of King Jesus, all those things will be complete.

The kingdom of God in its ultimate form is the literal, physical rule and reign of King Jesus on earth.

Until then, it's pain machine all the time.

So how do we live in this pain machine? What is our job? What is our duty?

---

4. *The primary mission of the people of God on planet earth is to save souls.*

This is how we make the world a better place. This is how we make our city a better place. Save souls. Bring people to Jesus.

- Social justice is not our Great Commission.
- Political involvement is not our Great Commission.
- Healing bodies is not our Great Commission.
- Signs and Wonders is not our Great Commission.
- Bible Study is not our Great Commission.

These things may be important and good in their place, no denying that. But I've been a Christian long enough to see us chase a million shiny things.

We might have many missions, but we have only one Great Commission.

Jesus saw the pain around him. He felt it deeply. He saw the injustice. He saw the inequality. He saw the unfairness. He saw the heartache. All of this touched him deeply.

And what was his solution?

And He said to them, "Go into all the world and preach the gospel to every creature." (Mark 16:15)

Christians will pray. Christians will study the Bible. Christians will run ministries for kids and for people in need and all that. Christians will gather to sing and worship.

That doesn't take much pushing from Christian leaders. But the first thing that dies in a church without constant reminders from leadership is evangelism. *Go get lost people saved!* That's what evangelism means. Poor people, rich people, drugged out people, sane people, all people. Because even if we can't restore Paradise on earth, till Jesus returns, we can restore hope in every human heart that believes.

We can restore marriages, so husbands and wives can live in harmony in the home. We can restore parenting, so children can be brought up in nurturing environments where life is precious and each individual's uniqueness is cherished. We can restore family units, churches, and neighborhoods, so that people feel the love and value they were created for. We can influence government and culture toward human respect, individual liberty, and moral decency.

The church changes the world one heart at a time. That's how Jesus did it. That's how his followers did it. That's how we're supposed to do it today.

Because only people who get saved will live forever, and dwell in that beautiful paradise called the millennial reign of Christ.

That is the mission we who name the name of Jesus share: the incredible honor of helping people find and follow God.

# SECULARISM

There's a word in Christian vocabulary that describes what we've been talking about throughout this book. It's the word *apologetics*. It sounds a lot like the word apology, but that's not what it means.

Apologetics simply means giving a defense of what you believe. Christian apologetics is a big deal to me. I believe in it. I believe that there has never been a world view that offers so much as the Christian world view.

There has never been a worldview more logical. There has never been a worldview more life-affirming. There has never been a worldview as consistent, as true to experience, as health-giving to the human psyche, and as beautiful as the biblical Christian world view. There's nothing like it. There's nothing even close.

I say that the message of Jesus Christ, that the truths of the laws and teachings of Scripture, and the story of the Old Rugged Cross, really need no defending.

## A BRIEF RANT

It is not the proclaimers of Jesus Christ who should be making a defense of the faith — God's truth is self-authenticating.

How did we Christians ever allow ourselves to be knocked into a defensive position?

No, it is the proclaimers of the heartbreaking, logic-defying, soul-deadening, reality-denying illusions of our age — they're the ones who should be defending their faith.

Where is their apologetics? Where is their defense of their calloused faith?

How does the atheist defend a beginning without a beginner?

How can the evolutionist defend natural selection in the face of the irreducible complexity of molecular machines like the flagellum?

How can a so-called humanist ever defend the movement in Iceland to abort all Down Syndrome babies?

A PhD director at Johns Hopkins just published an utterly appalling article arguing the utterly indefensible position: "Science proves kids are bad for earth. Morality suggests we should stop having them." He goes on to say that humans are bad for earth, and makes the moral case that we should have fewer humans.

How many fewer? This is indefensible, yet it is the gospel of the depopulation movement. It sickens those who cherish human life.

How can any thinking human being with a mind or a conscience defend this position? It is not humanism. It is inhumanism. It is a defense of cruelty. It is the most deadly position you can take. It is eugenics. It is naziism. It is hatred of what God calls sacred. Where are their apologetics for that?

It is the secularists who have an indefensible position.

How can you defend today's heartbreaking ethic of sexuality when it divorces the sexual act from any permanent emotional bond, and turns us all into sexual animals?

Can you defend that? Where are your apologetics books and conferences for the benefits of unbridled sexual expression?

You have none, because you cannot make your case.

All you can do is shake your fist at ours.

But that's okay, God is strong. And long after the critics have exhausted themselves, God's truth will endure.

The Bible is an anvil that has worn out many hammers.

The only quality that defines these opponents to biblical Christianity is that they are opposed to biblical Christianity. Other than that, they have absolutely nothing constructive to offer. They are derivative. They are intellectually exhausted. They see no need to defend their unfaith, because they have taken the intellectually lazy course of assuming their case to be true.

Atheistic, secularized, humanism isn't a movement and never will be. This is why it cannot hold big conferences or attract crowds. It is an un-movement. All it can do is deconstruct biblical Christianity—the most positive, beautiful, constructive force the world has ever known.

The Bible says...

And for this reason God will send them strong delusion, that they should believe the lie. (2 Thessalonians 2:11)

Strong delusion. That is what we see today.
Believing a lie.
Illusions.
The Matrix.

Recently, I took part in a speaker's conference in San Jose, the heart of Silicon Valley. It was a great experience, but the pastor told me something pretty sad.

Only two percent of people in Silicon Valley are part of a church. Ninety-eight percent are so lost that they do not know their spiritual right hand from their spiritual left. They are the brightest of the bright when it comes to technology and the digital world. Yet they are numb to the God who made them and holds their breath in his hands.

They have fallen hook line and sinker for the illusion of secularism.

## WHAT IS SECULARISM?

*Secularism is what happens when nice people live decent lives without meaningful reference to God.*

Secularism does not mean a person is anti-God. It doesn't not mean a person is an atheist. It does not mean a person is evil or a bad person. It simply means that God is left out of the picture of their lives in any meaningful way.

The word secular comes from the Latin word for the opposite of church. It means unchurchy. Worldly. Godless.

Secular is the opposite of sacred.

Secular people would describe themselves as spiritual. They would say they are good people, and they are. They would care about a few important causes. And they might be loving people and really good friends.

They are simply devoid of Jesus, the Bible, and God in their everyday lives.

By this definition, a whole lot of Americans would fit the profile of secularism. A whole lot of Christians would too — at least in their everyday mode of operation. Nice people, decent lives, with minimal reference to God.

## WHAT ARE SOME FEATURES OF SECULARISM?

*DRIFTED NOT DECIDED: Secular people drift into a god-free existence without much thinking about it.*

If this is you, you probably just drifted into your philosophy of life. You didn't study much. Didn't really weigh the options. You might have even avoided the topic of religion on purpose. Too divisive.

If you're being brutally honest, too intrusive. Who wants a God running their life, right?

Plus you're busy with all the stuff of life.

Jesus told a parable about it:

Jesus replied with this illustration: "A man prepared a great feast and sent out many invitations. When all was ready, he sent his servant around to notify the guests that it was time for them to come. But they all began making excuses. One said he had just bought a field and wanted to inspect it, so he asked to be excused. Another said he had just bought five pair of oxen and wanted to try them out. Another had just been married, so he said he couldn't come. (Luke 14:16-20)

Their answers were right away. Here comes this invitation. A lavish feast. The great master. Riches. Treasures. Blessings. Gifts.

None of that even makes a dent in their imaginations. They don't spend a second thinking about it.

This is pure secularism. They aren't bad people. They're just not interested in joining God's feast. It's probably a very nice feast, but there's other stuff to do. This other stuff isn't evil. It isn't bad. It isn't hurting anybody else.

But it is more important than the Master, so his invitation gets declined.

This is unthinking secularism. They just drifted into it.

And don't think it can't happen to you.

Can't you list a few people right now who used to be on fire for God, but now they don't have God in their lives at all? They drifted into it. Most likely, they didn't reject God intentionally. It wasn't the plan.

But now, every day God invites them to a feast of blessings, but... "I've got to take my kids to soccer, and I have a party to go to, and I have to fix my car, and I got a new boat and the lake is calling."

Good people. No longer God people.

Practical atheists.

―――――――

*DISCONTENT: Secularism, as a way of life, leaves your soul wanting more.*

There's always pain beneath the surface.

Something missing. An emotional hole the world can't fill.

A while back, when I was a youth and children's pastor, we had our big kids summer event. A packed house, and a bunch of kids on the stage.

One of the kids was really concerned about a man named Chuck. Chuck was dating this little boy's mom, and Chuck didn't know Jesus. He would be in the auditorium for our closing kids' program, and the little boy asked me if we could sing a song for Chuck, and dedicate it to him.

So we did. We got all the kids on stage, and before we sang this song, I announced that there was somebody here named Chuck, and though this song was for everybody, it was especially for Chuck.

This is what the kids sang that day:

> *The world will try to satisfy that deep*
> *longing in your soul,*

*You can search the whole world over, but*
*you'll be just as before.*
*You'll never find true satisfaction, until*
*you've found the Lord,*
*For only Jesus can satisfy your soul.*
*Only Jesus can satisfy your soul.*
*Only he can change your life, and make*
*you whole.*
*He'll give you peace you never knew,*
*Love and joy, and gladness too.*
*For only Jesus can satisfy your soul.*

— *[BY LANNY WOLFE]*

I should mention that Chuck was a member of a violent motorcycle gang.

I should also mention that Chuck put his personal faith in Jesus that day, and was made new by the grace of God.

No life is satisfying without God at the core. There is always sadness beneath the surface. Always fear. Always anxiety.

Secularism constricts you to a temporary existence — your soul was designed for an infinity of time and timelessness.

Secularism locks you into an earthly existence — your soul was made to soar in the heavenly realms.

Secularism reduces you to matter and energy — your whole being was made matter and energy, breathed into by the breath of God and created in his image.

Secularism glorifies the superficial toys of pleasure and prestige — when your whole being was crafted by God for eternal glories that words can't describe.

Money doesn't matter. Power doesn't matter. Popularity doesn't matter. Earthly prestige doesn't matter. None of these things can ultimately satisfy your soul.

And it is dysfunctional to keep on seeking satisfaction that way.

C.S. Lewis describes it perfectly:

"It would seem that Our Lord finds our desires not too strong, but too weak. We are half-hearted creatures, fooling about with drink and sex and ambition when infinite joy is offered us, like an ignorant child who wants to go on making mud pies in a slum because he cannot imagine what is meant by the offer of a holiday at the sea. We are far too easily pleased."

— [LEWIS, THE WEIGHT OF GLORY]

Because when you marginalize God, you shrink your life. You squeeze in the borders of your existence. And where God meant you to fly, you limp.

So that a secular life is a discontented life.

Which leads to the third feature:

---

*FRANTIC: Secularism drives a soul into a frantic search for happiness.*

> With the Lord's authority let me say this: Live no longer as the ungodly do, for they are hopelessly confused. Their closed minds are full of darkness; they are far away from the life of God because they have shut their minds and hardened their hearts against him. They don't care anymore about right and wrong, and they have given themselves over to immoral ways. Their lives are filled with all kinds of impurity and greed. (Ephesians 4:17-19, NLT)

This is a downward spiral.
A secular person can't escape it.

1. Rejection of Truth.
2. Spiritual Blackout.
3. Alienation from the life of God.
4. Moral Breakdown.
5. Calloused hearts (desensitized).
6. Sexual Brokenness (broken sense of self, attachment disorder, divorcing sex from attachment)

7. Greed, which is a Frantic Search for Happiness

I don't know what you think of when you hear the word Greed, but it's a really profound concept in the Bible, an inner mechanism of a broken soul.

Greed is a frantic search for happiness. It happens when what used to make you happy doesn't make you happy any more. So you need more if it. You kick the search for happiness into high gear, because the old stuff doesn't work any more.

There is a Law of Diminishing Returns.

The first time you try something, it's exciting. But after a while, the excitement wears off. So you have to double the dose. And for a while, the double dose is awesome. But you get used to that, and now you have to double the dose again. It's the law of diminishing returns. Each time you try a thing, you need more of the thing to make you happy.

It applies to pretty much everything. Sex. Money. Security. Relationships.

This is the birth of addiction.

This is all the secularized person has. The Law of Diminishing Returns is the driver of secular frustration, and it will never go away.

The world is never enough.

Since it is never enough, you're always grasping for more... more "mud pies" instead of the eternally satisfying feast of everyday life with God.

This is the spirit of the age. This is the default position of the typical person we hang out with every single day. They are satisfied on the surface, but deep down, they are desperate inside.

The conference I was at in San Jose met at a church. The pastor told me that so many people in these high tech companies look so good on the outside. But two things are true about them: a) they are shallow, he said. And, b) they are afraid. He said there's a reason they work eighty hours a week. They're always only one inch away from a life-changing job loss, so the pressure is relentless.

You might feel it too. We live in an age of Anxiety. It's crazy. It's irrational, its absurd. It is a colorless way to live, like watching black and white TV.

And it is today's normal.

But it isn't God's normal.

So what can we say to our secularized friends? It's simple: Try Jesus.

Why should they try Jesus?


## WHAT DO WE SAY TO SECULARIZED FRIENDS?

*1. Because EXCUSES < FORGIVENESS.*

The world offers an illusion of forgiveness. In the secular mind, sins are *excused*, but not truly forgiven. The offense has not been forgiven; it has just been redefined as not an offense. Excuses have been constructed. "That's okay," the offender is told. "You couldn't help yourself. It's no big deal. Nobody got hurt. Don't worry about it."

But the heart still remembers its guilt and shame no matter how many excuses get piled up.

Only Jesus meets you there, in that place, where you've offended, and hurt people, and taken advantage and sinned. He meets you with his true payment for your true guilt by his sacrificial death and shed blood on Calvary's Cross. And as a consequence of that, the debt is payed, the penalty is complete, and the forgiveness he brings is is the most reality-based, un-illusory, solid, lasting forgiveness a soul can claim.

Why? Because the sin has been paid in full by the blood of Christ. Where else can you find an atonement that actually atones?

Try Jesus.

---

*2. Because BROKENNESS < LOVE.*

The world offers an illusion of love. It settles for a two dimensional love that touches the body and the soul, but not the spirit. Jesus Christ came to give you a three dimensional, full-orbed love. He adds a supernatural dimension to every loving relationship that invites him in — but it's more than that.

*The truths Jesus taught can repair the broken places in your heart that get in the way of love.*

Let that settle in.

- The wounds that used to dominate you can be healed and lose their power.
- The memories that haunt you can be purified.
- The scars that mar your body and your soul can be overcome by the grace of Jesus.
- The lies that confused you can be corrected.
- The bitterness that infects every relationship.
- The displaced anger from a lifetime of hurt.

There is truth in Jesus Christ, and in his Word, to heal, to correct, to empower, and to set you free to the kind of bonds of affection that last, and to satisfy, and to fill your heart with joy.

Try Jesus.

---

### 3. Because COPING < COMFORT

Try Jesus, because under a secular worldview, the only answer to suffering is to cope.

But Jesus offers comfort not only now, but forever.

The Bible treats suffering as an alien invader. It was not part of God's original creation. Pain entered later, when sin and evil entered. No death, no sorrow, no suffering, and no pain existed in God's good creation. The biblical authors never blame God for the problem of pain. God didn't create evil or the suffering it birthed.

When sin galloped into the world, suffering and death rode in on its back. That was the free will choice of the human race.

But, Scripture reveals that God did not stand aloof from the problem of pain; he became human without ceasing to be God, and submerged himself in the depths of pain like no other human before or since.

When he died on the Cross, Jesus absorbed into himself, all the punishment, all the sorrows, all the pains, and all the condemnation all the darkness and evil of the world ever called down upon itself. It all landed in the heart of Jesus Christ. He felt its weight. He felt its darkness. Its lostness. Its hopelessness and despair. He felt it all. Which means…

God understands the problem of pain through direct experience. "Since he himself has gone through suffering and temptation, he is able to help us when we are being tempted" (Hebrews 2:18, NLT). No matter how much you hurt, you are never alone. God comes alongside you and is ready to embrace you with an empathy that knows no bounds.

No other worldview even comes close. No other God- became-man suffered and died as our sin-bearer. No other god satisfied the demands of cosmic justice relative to evil, while providing the final solution to the problem of pain.

Christianity offers the world a God who felt the fullest measure of human suffering, a Savior who comforts us in our suffering, a global mission to alleviate suffering, final justice for those who cause suffering, and a coming world that abolishes suffering.

Try Jesus, because he is the only comfort that lasts in a world gone crazy.

---

4. *Because SENSELESS CONTRADICTIONS < COHERENT TRUTHS.*

Western philosophy has evolved backwards. It has devolved. We have entered a stage where true can mean false and evil can mean good. It is irrational. It is contradictory.

How should Christians live in this craziness?

We have to grow to a point where we can say there is something called truth and it is knowable. It is knowable because truth stays true, no matter where you go, and no matter what the situation may be. And no matter who is looking at it.

We have only two choices. Either we can say that

what we are experiencing is real, OR we can say that everything is just a dream of a dream in the mind of a god, the fantasy of the matrix, or a computer running its code.

If you want a life grounded in reality, you have to start with these three basic ideas.

One. God is.

Two. God has spoken.

Three. God's speech is not nonsense.

That is the only way to escape irrationality. The philosophy of the world is utterly contradictory. It is unreality. It is absurd. It is logically inconsistent.

Remember the slide in a children's playground?

Irrationality is how you climb to the top. Absurdity is where you sit down. Surrender is the push that gets you going. Despair is in the middle. And self-destruction finds you at the bottom.

A great thinker of the World War 2 era, Dorothy Sayers, wrote:

*Theologically this country is at present in a state of utter chaos established in the name of religious toleration and rapidly degenerating into flight from reason and the death of hope.*

— (IN CREED OR CHAOS)

The whole statement, but particularly the

phrase, "flight from reason" perfectly describes the last half-century in America.

It describes the Internet. It describes government. Art. Music. Entertainment. Gaming. Monetary Policy. Morality. University systems. Everything.

A flight from reason.

The embrace of irrationality. A heap of messy contradictions embraced by all.

If we are simply a bag of impersonal matter and energy randomly mixed into a chemical soup through chance and random process, then there is no intelligence in the universe. No order. No transcendent truth. No love. No meaning. No purpose. Nothing to look forward to. Just the coming energy death of maximum entropy and the snuffing out of the light of life.

But if a Creator has made us, and spoken to us, then there is hope. And there is every likelihood he has spoken to us about ourselves.

That is the reason we can be made whole. It is the only reason.

Your heart is a finely tuned instrument, an intricate wonder, a marvel of emotions and multiple moving parts. The Maker has tuned you to the realities that matter most.

In the mind of God, the world makes sense.

When you share his mind, then your life, world, and even your loves begin to make sense. When you view your life from the vantage point of Mt. Eternity, you will see yourself as the masterpiece-in-progress that you really are.

This is because truth fits with truth. And because, when you share the mind of Christ, you see the heart-pounding beauty of the whole of God's breathtaking creation.

*Truth matters because love matters.*

*Love requires trust.*

*Trust requires truth.*

Truth matters because love matters.

My prayer for you and me and all of us is that we might escape the matrix, step out of the dream, shed the illusions, and plant our feet on the bedrock of the magnificent truth that is found in Christ Jesus our Lord.

That is the way to the abundant life Jesus promised.

That is the way to joy.

# ACKNOWLEDGEMENTS

As always, a book takes a village, and I
   am privileged to be part of a
   good one.

First and foremost, I am grateful to be the
   husband of Margi Giovannetti,
   friend, partner, genius, lawyer,
   designer, creative, and analyst
   extraordinaire. You make me a better
   man, a better Christian, and a better
   writer.

My kids, Josie and JD make me proud to
   be alive. Keep the faith and always
   and forever keep your heart warm
   and tender toward Christ.

I am ever grateful to my writer buddy,
   Dave Meurer, for dragging me into
   this world of authorship.

*I owe a big debt of gratitude to my agent,
Janet Grant, and to the the Books &
Such Literary Management team for
constant insight and inspiration.
I am especially thankful to Meridith
Chase for your expert proofreading
and continual encouragement.
To God be the glory.*